Celeste Gonzales

foreword by Lori Champion

YOU ARE NOT WHO YOU *think* YOU ARE

Just do it!
Celesta ♡
Joshua 1:9

THINK DIFFERENT
BREAK CYCLES
Be CONFIDENT

Dedication

To the love of my life, Daniel: You placed value on me the day we locked eyes at fifteen years old. This book would not have been written without the healing love you have lavished me with for the last twenty plus years. I know Jesus better because of you. Thank you for the countless hours of encouraging me as I penned this book. You embraced me in the tearful moments and had patience when the laundry was at the bottom of my to-do list. Above all else, you believed in my dream for ten years as God wrote this book in my heart. Thank you for never giving up on me. I love you with everything! You are my valiant knight, and I will forever be your precious pearl.

To my kids Syrena, Luke and Kya: You are my joy. When I wake up and go to bed, you are on my mind. I rejoice in the distinct gifts each of you have been given. I often think of how I don't deserve to have such a wonderful family, but I'm so grateful that God does not give us what we deserve. My heart for each of you is to serve the Lord all your lives and become exactly who God has called you to be. I pray this book inspires you to overcome any obstacles you will face in life, knowing that God is for you, He is faithful and He is good. No matter what, remember that Mommy loves you, Daddy loves you, Jesus loves you and Jesus wants to be your friend forever.

To my dad, James: Thank you. You've loved me through every hurt and pain we both had to walk through. Growing up, I dreamed of being a daddy's girl, and I am living that dream. I look forward to our at random hour-long phone conversations, Tuesday walks and out of the blue text encouragements. As I shared with you the contents and vulnerability of this book, you welcomed it; you even brought more insight, healing and strength to our relationship. The day I sent my book off to be prepared for publishing was an emotional one. I told you it was like I had sent off a lifetime of pain and victory. You responded, "Now it will be someone else's victory!" Thank you for being my constant support through the process of writing this book. There's been no greater example in my life of God's extravagant love than the love you've showed me! I love you, Daddy!

To my loving mother, Sylvia: Thank you. You named me with such distinction, knowing the many messages I would be asked to deliver throughout my life. Thank you for loving me in and through all things. Growing up, I saw you as a fierce warrior that feared nothing, yet also as a beautiful, gentle dove. Thank you for teaching me how to be a strong woman that can stay tender in her love and care for others. You will always be my rock, my prayer warrior, and my faithful friend. I love you, Mom!

To my mother-in-love, Lena: You are my biggest fan! You read my book in two days, hanging on every word. When I'm with you, my value instantly increases with your affection. Your prayers have strengthened me and given me the power to boldly do what God has called me to do. Thank you for believing in me and for your love and support. You are more than a mother-in-law, you are my dearest friend.

To my sisters by birth and by choice: I love you with all of my heart. What a gift I have in you and your consistent love and kindness toward me. You are each my forever friends, which is more than I could ever deserve. Thank you for reading my book (multiple times) and for helping me to process through hard spaces. Thank you for encouraging me when I wanted to give up. You are my most loyal and trustworthy companions. I'm so thankful we get to grow old together.

To the Brents, aka my second family: Thank you for giving me a safe space to be known and loved. You are each near and dear to my heart. You have built a strong fortress, a home that heals. Your friendship has been living waters to my family. There is none like you! Monica, you are a gift from God that I cherish. This story would not have been written without you.

To Andrea: You have walked with me in every season, and our friendship has grown all the more. Thank you for reading every word of this book more than once! Your encouragement to me gave me the confidence to continue to move forward. You are a faithful friend, and I deeply value you!

To Joe and Lori Champion: Thank you my beloved pastors. You saw in me what I could not see for myself: value and purpose. You called potential out of my life and entrusted me beyond anything I ever thought I could do. You've pastored me through every hard space I've walked through, always believing God's best for me. You cheered me on through this book project, and your belief in me made me believe in myself. Thank you for marking me as loved.

In loving memory of Mel Davis: Your choice to live a holy and set apart life afforded me the prophetic words of healing you spoke to me so many years ago. The title of this book is written from those words. I know heaven called you home, but your impact on Earth and in my heart will forever remain. Thank you.

In loving memory of Robert Gonzales: Dad, your last words to me were to not be afraid of what God would ask me to do. Your words often echo in my ear. I miss you, but I know you are exactly where you wanted to be and receiving your eternal reward. Thank you for accepting me when I felt rejected and making room in the family to receive me. I love you and will see you in heaven.

Contents

Foreword

If anyone (especially a new author) ever hands you the manuscript of their book, realize you have been entrusted with the raw version of their blood, sweat and tears. Really, it's sometimes the unseen and unedited parts of their lives. Book-writing is therapeutic; you dig deep into places that have often been covered, left behind and forgotten for years.

My friend and long-time colaborer in ministry, Celeste, not only handed me her manuscript, but in the pocket of the three-ring-binder was an ink pen. An ink pen. She said, "Take out whatever you think needs to go." I edited nothing out. I used that ink pen to draw stars and check marks and wrote "Great point" and "100" throughout the God-inspired and thoughtfully written pages. I can't escape the inner elementary teacher that I still am!

The curse and the blessing of leadership is that you often see the potential of people before they see it in themselves. The curse part is you watch and try to coach them into their purpose, but many will never get out of their own way and do the hard things to get themselves to the other side of what holds them back. The blessing of leadership is when someone not only lives up to what you see as their potential, but they live beyond it, through the power of Christ and through their commitment to growth and discipleship, and allow the pains and insufficiencies of their past to be redeemed.

In 2003, this twenty-two-year-old girl and her husband walked into our storefront church, and she would barely look me in the eye. She would have preferred to work in the nursery (not because she had a passion for kids, but because she wanted to be hidden), and now she leads and proclaims God's Word to thousands of people, leads our women's conference in Texas, in women's prisons, and around the world. As a leader who sees potential in people, I hate to admit this, but even I didn't see all of that in the young woman who wouldn't make eye contact with me almost two decades ago. I definitely saw more in her than what she was showing at the time, but not the above-and-beyond doors that God would open to her.

The difference is this: Few people hand the manuscript of their lives to God or to others with an ink pen included. People ask God to mold them and make them, then say, "Nevermind" when it actually requires something of them that they want to hold onto or when it causes them to step out of limitations that comfort them.

I've had a front row seat to the journey documented on the pages of this book. No, this is not an autobiography of Celeste. It's a story of how to trust God with everything so that you can become more than anyone else, including you, could have ever imagined.

—Lori Champion
Author of *Woman UP*
Co-Pastor of Celebration Church

Introduction

At forty I finally wrote this book; in fact, I finished it the day before my forty-first birthday. I've had it in my heart a long time, but the truth is I haven't always liked who I was . . . Or who I thought I was . . . Or who I was told I was. When I was thirty-one, after a season of betrayal, a pastor, who knew nothing about my situation, began to pray and prophesy over me. Among many other things, he said, "You are not who you think you are. You are what God thinks of you!" He concluded with, "God wants your thoughts concerning yourself to come up a notch." I'm not sure if you've ever had negative thoughts about yourself or allowed the opinions of others to draft a very small image and future for you, but for me, every day was challenged with these condemning notions. The words spoken over me by that pastor gave me permission to change the scenery in my mind and the trajectory of my future.

As kids, I think most of us felt like there was something great, something unique, something special about who we were and who we were meant to become. But life has a way of shrinking our God-sized dreams into laughable, unbelievable, unattainable fairytales. Well, I'm here to tell you, "You're not who you think you are!" God has made you for greatness, and whether you're fifteen or well past fifty, it's not too late to become the hero you've always wanted to be.

At the beginning of the pandemic of 2020, I asked God, "What do you want my response to be to all of this?" He impressed on my heart to "Be the hero you've always wanted to be." Now that was exciting for me because I'm a Marvel fan, but what I realized is that heroes are not forged in an hour-and-a-half movie.

We all hope that when we are faced with adversity, we will rise to the occasion, but I believe that in those moments of fight or flight what's already inside of us will be what's on display for all to see. So what's inside of you? When you take a deeper look into your life, what is it that you see? Do you see someone who is confident or someone who is a coward? Do you see boldness or do you see an array of fears? Do you see beauty or do you see pain? Do you see potential or do you see complacency?

Heroes are not born, they are developed.

If you don't see what you want to see, that's OK, because heroes are not born, they are developed. They are developed by the small, daily, unseen and sometimes mundane decisions and habits that breed consistency, clarity and confidence. If we are faithful in doing the hard things—steward our hearts, correct our habits and become women who reflect the character and nature of our loving God—then God will be faithful and do the impossible when we are faced with moments of heroism!

I once hated to look in the mirror. I said horrible things to myself, and I nurtured and protected every harsh and critical word ever spoken to me like it was a precious jewel. I became what I hated because I believed the worst of myself. In doing so, I gave myself no grace or space for the relentless redemption of my Lord and Savior, Jesus Christ. Oh . . . but He is the Hero above all heroes, and He continued to seek me and was faithful to save me. This book is here pursuing you, for you are not who you think you are, and it is my honor to share God's heart in the matter with you. May my journey be a source of hope and a key that unlocks some truths that will transform your heart to be whole and be freed to enjoy the person God has created you to be!

Do Identity Versus Be Identity

One thing I've noticed recently is how much we have made our identities center on what we do. Test this theory out for yourself the next time you go to a dinner party. When you meet someone new, within the first five minutes of your conversation, see if you or your new acquaintance says these four words: "What do you do?" A friend shared with me that while she was between jobs and unsure of her next career path, she avoided all places where she'd be asked this question because it made her feel so small. She had so many amazing and interesting qualities that made up her person, but none of that was weighed, measured or valued in the metaphorical "do" identity. The mirror said everything was great and beautiful, but inside she longed for identity and purpose.

In those instances, we need maturity to develop our thinking and grab ahold of the truth that who we are is so much more than what we do. Sure, some of what we do is an outpouring of who we have become, much like true faith will be followed by works. But I can do a lot of things that simply don't add to my character, like the laundry for instance. But say I do the laundry for a friend that just had surgery, that does speak to who I am. Where we get it mixed up is when we try to "do" Christianity. What does that even mean? We can't possibly "do" any one thing twenty-four hours a day, seven days a week, and we certainly can't fight a real devil as a part-time Christian!

So instead of doing Christianity, we need to *be* Christian. The foundation of our identity is to become like Christ so we can reflect his image; thus, we have to "be." Who I am doesn't stop when I sleep, make a mistake, change careers or go for a grocery run! Consider Israel who had lived as slaves for over four hundred years. If who they were only depended on what they did as slaves, it would just be a sad story of harsh labor. We would not understand their rich heritage or their overcoming spirit, and we certainly would not accept the reality that Jesus, the creator of the universe, was born through their lineage. Looking at the story of their lives, we see the depth of character they had and the process of becoming they embraced and at times rejected.

Who you are is not what you do. Our identity is secure in the unchanging nature of the One who created us. This should give us peace because no matter what season we find ourselves in, we can have great confidence in who we are in Christ. If you truly want to do big things in your life, you are first going to have to learn how to just *be!*

What to Expect in this Book

This book, alongside some epic biblical tales, is paved with thirteen *BE* qualities adopted from my own journey of discovering who I am. My hope through these pages is that you will be equipped to apply the principles shared, so your reflection will accurately depict a becoming you love. Each chapter of this book will give you a *BE* characteristic to adopt in your own development of your identity to help you remember who you are.

Growing up my mom would always tell me, "Remember who you are!" as I walked out the door. The problem was, I had no idea who I was. I thought when Jesus handed out gifts and talents, He accidentally skipped over me in the metaphorical line. Truth be told, Jesus never makes mistakes, including you, your personality and maybe even your gifts that you sometimes see as burdens. God is perfect, so we can trust His workmanship.

If our view of God is wrong, our reflection of ourselves will always be blurry.

If our view of God is wrong, our reflection of ourselves will always be blurry.

During our time together I will provoke thought that will

challenge the narrow lens through which you've viewed your past, present and future. If you want to really see change in your life, you will have to choose to be honest in these moments that will expose areas of your life that have hindered you. Honesty will give you the opportunity to receive healing and activate energy to live a life without regret. At the end of each chapter, give yourself time to reflect on what you've read and invite the Holy Spirit to bring clarity to chaotic places of your soul.

I've penned these words for someone, like you, who is willing to do the hard work to heal. Come on this journey with me, friend.

My Reflections

"Without reflection, we go blindly on our way, creating more unintended consequences, and failing to achieve anything useful."

-Margaret J. Wheatley

For now we see in a mirror dimly, but then face to face. Now I know in part; then I shall know fully, even as I have been fully known.

1 Corinthians 13:12 (ESV)

Chapter 1
Be Whole

Here's the truth: our reflection only tells us a part of the story. It only shows us the scars, the bruises, the outward beauty, the wanted or unwanted curls, the dimples we show off or the ones we try to hide. . . . The mirror shows a lot, but it is not the *whole* story. In this book we are going to face the truth about ourselves, so we might see the beauty in our reflection either for the first time or maybe once again. The "me" that I see in the mirror today is much different than the "me" I often reflect upon. My hope is that after reading this book, you will realize that you are not who you think you are, you are what God thinks of you. I truly believe that He wants your thoughts concerning yourself to come up a notch.

What We Choose to Believe

My perspective

Growing up, looking into a mirror was not a positive experience for me. What I saw was all my "nots": not pretty, not smart and not wanted. I have photos where I can see the emptiness behind my smile and the negative thoughts behind my eyes. I come from God-fearing, loving parents, but even in a good home, you can experience hurt.

My entire childhood I remember my parents laughingly sharing the story of how I came to be. Just about fifteen months after having my sister, my mom discovered that she was surprisingly pregnant with me. I can imagine her standing at the door waiting for my dad to come home from work so she could share the good news. My mom was a young mom, only twenty-one at the time, and pregnant with baby number two. I'm sure she was filled with excitement and nerves all at the same time.

When my dad came home from work, my mom blurted out the news, "I'm pregnant!" Unfortunately, my dad's response was less than excited. In fact, he didn't say a word to her. He looked at her stunned and then turned around and walked out the door. I can only imagine how my mom felt standing there with no idea what my dad was thinking or when he would come back inside to give her any kind of response. After what seemed like a long time of silence, he finally walked back in the door, and the only solace he found in the fact that they were pregnant again was that this time he would get a boy. Well, we all know how that turned out!

Although only two years apart, my sister and I looked more like twins than big sis and little sis. She was super small for her age because of some health challenges, and I grew very fast, so by the time we were two and four years old, we were sharing clothes! My dad would jokingly call me "Fatty Patty," always teasing me about my size. To him it was endearing, but as I grew older, these labels and seemingly innocent stories invited me to buy the lie that I was not wanted and that I was ugly. Never hearing that I was beautiful at home left me to my own demeaning thoughts, and the narrative that I played in my mind was grim. I held those thoughts deep in my soul, and I protected them and let the enemy nurture them until they became my identity.

When I was six years old, my little sister was born and brought completion to our family of five. I loved her, as we all did; however, the struggles I was having with finding my place in our family just continued to grow. I wasn't the oldest with all the accolades and privileges, and I wasn't the youngest being catered to. There is certainly a truth to the theories held around being a middle child. I had a constant feeling of being overlooked and unseen.

As I grew older, I discovered that bad bread was better than no bread when you are hungry, and I was starving for affirmation. Boys took notice of me at a young age, and I would fall for any guy that said the right things to me. Because of this, I found myself on a rollercoaster of constant breakups and boyfriends, chasing affirmation and giving more and more of myself away with every worthless exchange. I embodied a new false sense of control. I wouldn't stay with anyone long enough for them to reject me. I felt as though I had to be in charge of the image I wanted to protect, even if it didn't reflect the truth of the insecurities I held inside.

At eighteen an on-again-off-again boyfriend proposed to me, and I said yes. I wanted out of my situation. I wanted security. I wanted to feel loved. At a family dinner, we decided to share the good news, and when we did, my dad responded, in front of everyone, "Why would you ever want to marry her?" Heartbroken and humiliated, I barely held it together through the dinner. The walls of insecurity that had been layered brick by brick in my heart were fortified that day. I resolved to self-protect because from my perspective no one else would bring me shelter from such excruciating pain.

A profound fear that I had cradled under the surface until this point was unleashed to run wild in my mind: "You are not lovable." I had heard it before lingering in my thoughts, but I had always been able to hold it at bay. Now it was out in the open, plain and simple for everyone to see.

Most of us can relate on some level to the feelings of rejection. Maybe reading my story even brought up some harsh and critical words that were said to you. Things like:

- ♥ Who could ever love you?
- ♥ I wish you had never been born.
- ♥ You are ugly.
- ♥ You are stupid.
- ♥ You will never amount to anything.

Although hurtful words were said to us, they do not have to be validated by us. I can distinctly remember repeating discriminating voices over and over in my head, especially when a mirror was involved. I gave my emotions permission to take the lead when I received any type of correction or criticism, resulting in a victim mindset. Using words like "I always . . ." or "You never . . ." when thinking of myself or others affirmed every hurtful word and excused my own bad behavior because of them. I wasn't whole in my understanding so I couldn't comprehend that we can be emotionally aware without being emotionally driven.

Although hurtful words were said to us, they do not have to be validated by us.

We can be emotionally aware without being emotionally driven.

The truth is, words are powerful and they can pierce us, but standing alone, these words are often a dim view of a greater story. We cannot take everything at face value. Our stories are important, but what's even more important is the lens through which we tell these stories. Young, eighteen-year-old eyes can't hold a holistic perspective.

Here's a fact: I was no picnic to raise! The pain that I was fostering in private came out in some pretty ugly ways through my words and through my rebellion toward my parents. Much of my regret in life is that I was not honest with how I felt. I did not know how to articulate the things I was holding inside. By hiding hurts, I left my parents to lead me in the dark, causing me to wound the people I loved the most. What about you? Is there a part of your story that you leave out because it's hard to admit or because you haven't investigated the other side? Could those findings radically shape your narrative to see things differently and even possibly live differently?

The other side

With matured eyes, I can see that my parents had walked through a really tough year the year my sister was born. She had health issues, and the reality that I was coming along sooner than they had planned brought them a lot of fear. I can imagine they were battling thoughts like, "Could this baby have health challenges also?" "How are we going to pay for another child?" My parents were living paycheck to paycheck at the time, and they were drowning in debt, barely getting by.

My dad recently shared with me that he often looks back at his response to my mom's announcement with regret of his own. He said that he allowed the fear of not being able to provide for his family to steal a moment of joy he and my mom should have been able to hold dear forever. If we are being honest, I think we all hold moments in our minds where we wish we could have a do-over!

Additionally, my parents had no idea that their continued praise of my sister and her healing story and sharing the unexpectedness of my arrival and its narrative made me feel like she was the miracle and I was the mess-up, the mistake.

The opposite was actually true! My sister had such a rough first year due to her health that it was miserable for everyone, but when I came along, I was the happiest, carefree little one, and it was a redeeming time for my parents. But the enemy sure didn't want me to hear that, so he prompted me to see the situation through a rejection filter. It's amazing to me how twisted and distorted the enemy can make you see things when you wear a rejection filter.

Changing Your Filter

When a filter is used, it holds back impurities. The type of filter we use will determine what we ingest. Let's also not forget that filters must be replaced to be effective. Have you ever let your air filter in your home go past its expiration date? I have, and it's disgusting and renders the filter useless. Not changing your filter, when maturing, can cause you to consume toxic air that is detrimental to your spirit and soul. We can breathe in a toxic understanding of who we are and who God is, or we can replace our filters with a matured understanding of who we are through God's full acceptance and love! It's time for change so we can breathe effortlessly.

Filters must be replaced to be effective.

The night of my proposal dinner, my dad said some of the most hurtful words that pierced me, but were they altogether accurate in my recollection? Admittedly frustrated, my dad recalls his tone being one of a concerned father inquiring as to this boy's intentions with me, not a careless blow to my worth.

We both remember the night vividly, yet still somehow have different perceptions and emotions surrounding it. Now, as a mother of three myself, I can see why my dad was agitated by the whole situation. He was undoubtedly annoyed by the lack of wisdom that my nineteen-year-old "fiancé" had in his timing to "ask" for my hand in marriage (after he had already proposed) in mixed company, at Chili's of all places. Not to mention the on-again-off-again relationship we had modeled since middle school! This was not the table talk any of us had envisioned for that night.

No matter what was said, or how it was said, in my dad's heart, he knew this was not the boy for me. He rightfully believed that if we moved forward, the marriage would likely end in divorce, something he never wanted me to go through. He wanted the best for his beloved daughter, but his daughter did not know his heart. The same can be true for our heavenly Father. If we don't accurately know His heart and His thoughts toward us, we can misinterpret moments of protection as moments of rejection.

In times of pain, we don't reason intellectually. Instead, we irrationally make judgements that support our emotions and insecurities. Pain experienced in the midst of our brokenness does not allow us to distinguish truth from lies. If we're secure, we can speak to our emotions by deductive reasoning and filter everything said through the truth of who God says we are. God's truth enables us to rationalize what was said versus what was meant, what can grow us versus what can harm us, what to hold and what to throw away. In contrast, insecurity has no room for grace or the other side of things, and it never gives us any responsibility in it all. Pain sheds light on where we are healed and places we still need to become whole.

One particular day, in my early thirties, I had a rough day at work. I got in my car and cried. I heard the Holy Spirit tell me

Insecurity has no room for grace or the other side of things, and it never gives us any responsibility in it all.

to go to my dad's house. That was the last place I wanted to go! Nevertheless, I showed up unannounced. While sitting on my dad's couch, I said, "Dad, I don't know why I'm here. I had a really hard day at work, and for whatever reason, the whole situation triggered me to feel like I was fifteen again." My dad looked at me and said, "Celeste, can I apologize to you? I have grieved at the loss of relationship with you." The father that I thought didn't want me had grieved for me. That day changed everything for our relationship: my perspective began to shift and my heart began to heal.

Looking back, through a filter of wisdom, I'm grateful for my childhood. There were *many* heroic moments that my parents played throughout my life, and most importantly, they gave me a foundation in Christ. Of course, none of this lessens the pain I experienced at the time. Please hear me when I say that there are things in my past and yours that cannot be rationalized away, as they were hurtful, whether they were done maliciously or in ignorance, but can we season them with grace? Can we marinate them in forgiveness that likely needs to be shared two ways? Can we determine in our heart to overcome them with redemption that consumes every bad intent and turns it into good?

A Dim View

Mirrors were created to aid us in our grooming process, but I would venture to say that they have vastly impaired our sight instead of improving it, imploring us to criticize, belittle and pick ourselves apart. When was the last time you looked in the mirror and said, "Hello, Gorgeous!" or "Girl, you age like fine wine!" Mirrors change our moods. We may be feeling fine, but then we glance in a mirror, which causes us to focus on ourselves and it negatively impacts our state of mind. And many times, mirrors are just not honest. Think about that department store mirror that made you look so amazing in that dress, then you got home and discovered it was all a lie! Reflections can reveal a pretty picture that is not necessarily true, but they can also reveal truths that are not necessarily a pretty picture.

> Reflections can reveal a pretty picture that is not necessarily true, but they can also reveal truths that are not necessarily a pretty picture.

In the spirit of vulnerability, here's an honest view of my thirtieth birthday. I wasn't looking forward to it. I didn't want a party, as I didn't want to celebrate. The fact is, I didn't want to face it. I was not where I wanted to be, and more deeply, I wasn't who I thought I should be at this juncture in my life. I still saw the same disappointment each time I would look into the mirror. No matter the promotions I had received, the value my husband placed on me or the wonderful family I had, my thoughts concerning myself stole every ounce of beauty and worth.

I woke up that birthday morning feeling unusually sore and achy. I didn't think too much about it, and then I looked in the mirror, and with everything in me, I wanted to scream! Dark circles. Bags under my eyes so deep I could have taken a ten-day trip to Cozumel. I thought, "I guess that's it. This is what thirty looks like." I wanted to crawl back into my bed with a gallon of ice cream! But . . . emotional breakdown or not, I was still a mom, so I went on with the day, only to be both relieved and annoyed by the discovery that this wasn't the new me. I just had the flu!

For now we see in a mirror, dimly . . .
1 Corinthians 12:12 (ESV)

You see, the mirror is a dim view of a greater story. The deeper you look, the more it reveals. My thirty-year-old self had not yet taken the courageous steps to look more intently into the spaces of pain that I had experienced in my youth. I had yet to sit on my father's couch and hear the words of healing my heart longed for, but my time came, and that time of healing is coming for you too.

The Bible is filled with compilations of historic accounts that compel us to take a deeper look. The account of Israel is one that shows us how we become whole and how to see a reflection that brings us confidence and maturity.

The people of Israel were miraculously freed from slavery because God both heard and answered their prayers. I love that God doesn't just hear us and leave it at that, but He answers us. As a response to their deliverance in Exodus 25, Israel began to build the tabernacle, a house for the Lord to dwell in. When you have been liberated from such cruelty, your heart longs to honor, worship, seek and hear from the One who has set you free!

Each person was asked to bring an offering from their heart to see this huge initiative accomplished. The women showed up big time. In my experience, women tend to show up big in times of crisis and need. During COVID-19, my sisters by blood and by choice lavished each other with phone calls, meals, surprise packages, drive-by parties—nothing could keep us from relationship or care in the midst of crisis. The women of Israel were no exception:

> They made the bronze basin and its bronze stand from the mirrors of the women who served at the entrance to the tent of meeting. Exodus 38:8 (NIV)

At a closer look, this text indicates to us that the only group of people who were recognized for their specific gift given were the women who served at the entrance of the church. The gift that they brought was important to their history, and it was equally important to their futures. They gave their mirrors.

These mirrors were different from what you and I are used to. They were bronze mirrors that gave a blurry, unclear reflection. Contemplate this gift for one moment. The serving women of the church gave up their mirrors; they gave up their dim view of how they saw themselves to build the house of God. Let that sink in . . .

We must give up the dim view of how we see ourselves to build the house of God.

Giving up this mirror meant saying goodbye to a reflection of themselves that was built in bondage. It's a freeing thought to no longer see the slave, but I wonder how many times, when they went back home, they reached for their mirror forgetting that they had given it away. Have you ever deleted an app from your phone because it's been stealing your time or disturbing your peace, only to find yourself picking up your phone to scroll and remembering it's no longer there? You gave it up, yet it's still calling you, pulling you to give it more of yourself. In our reflection, we can still see the slave, but God has come to free the slave:

In our reflection, we can still see the slave, but God has come to free the slave.

It is for freedom that Christ has set us free. Stand firm, then, and do not let yourselves be burdened again by a yoke of slavery. Galatians 5:1 (NIV)

A Mature Perspective

We had just moved, and for Mother's Day, my kids bought me some beautiful flowers. My daughter took the roses and placed them in a charming vase and carried it over to the sink to add some water. When she did, this seemingly fine vessel began to burst, spewing water everywhere. The bottom of the vase completely broke off! We didn't realize it had cracked on the inside during the move. It looked fine, but it wasn't. You see, something that is broken from the inside cannot hold weighty things. It can look pretty, but it cannot be useful! You can look fine and not be fine. You can fake it through life but then break under the mildest pressure.

So often we are broken on the inside from an immature perspective of ourselves. As someone who has walked through extensive seasons of healing, bringing me into wholeness (and trust me, I haven't arrived), I have a new perspective! I have a redeemed perspective. I have a perspective that is spiritually mature, and it started with my thinking.

> *When I was a child, I spoke like a child,*
> *I thought like a child, I reasoned like a child.*
> *When I became a man, I gave up childish ways.*
> *1 Corinthians 13:11 (ESV)*

I have a choice in how I speak, think and reason. It doesn't change what happened to me, how I felt or how I responded, but it can change who I am today. So much of how we see ourselves is shaped by our first eighteen years of life, but we get to decide who we become. Too many of us are walking around forty years old but feeling fifteen inside.

Our view of ourselves is shaped by the experiences we have in our first eighteen years of life, but we get to decide who we become.

You may be fifty, but when someone at work says something to you, it triggers shameful memories from when you were nine, causing you to retaliate or retreat.

For years, I would look in the mirror and think I was fat and ugly. Anyone that knows me and my petite stature would completely laugh at the notion, but for me, it was so real for so long. Still today, I have the choice to believe those lies that I nurtured for so long, or I can realize that the enemy manipulated my interpretation of my dad's voice to deceive my impressionable heart.

I can effortlessly accept that I'm not lovable or I can choose to remember who I am! I'm a Gonzales. For more than half my life, I have been loved by my affectionate husband, who pursues me still and tells me every day that I'm beautiful and wanted. More importantly, I am deeply loved by God as His beloved daughter. He gave everything for me just as He gave everything to display His love for you. We have a choice in where we will root our identity. I now choose to look to God to clearly see me. I may have played into those ugly stories of my past at one time, but I don't have to watch those tired reruns anymore! It's not worth the real estate in my mind. Why would I choose to live out of any lesser understanding of who I am?

It seems silly, but on the occasion these critical thoughts creep into my head and I've allowed them to stay there, it's because it was too much work to change the narrative. It takes being intentional to listen to God's voice instead of the false identity the enemy wants to place on you. It's a challenge to learn to discern which voice you are hearing and then speak back to

Speak back to what's speaking to you. what's speaking to you. It's like potty training a puppy: sometimes you've got to grab un-welcomed thoughts mid-flow and run them out the door before they make a mess in your home!

Where are you at? Do you want to continue to nurture the wounding words that were spoken to you so many years ago, or do you want to be whole? It's time. It's time to put the childish thinking away. It's time to grow up. It's time to heal. The lie that was seeded in you so many years ago is laughable to anyone who knows you. Just as you would roll your eyes at me for thinking of some of the things I've shared, you too have taken cheap bait that completely conflicts with your character!

God wants to heal the girl that's inside of the woman. You are so much more than what happened to you. Freely, Christ has given to us the power to be emancipated from the chains of shame, inadequacy, history, comparison, rejection and fear by accepting the full love of God *God wants to heal the girl that's inside of the woman.* and by receiving the truth of who He has made us to be. We can reflect His image and be made whole from the inside out.

The Becoming

One night, I was feeling particularly annoyed; basically, I was in a mood! Have you ever had one of those? I was in sweats, a

T-shirt, messy bun, no makeup and standing in the kitchen at the end of the day, and my husband couldn't keep his hands off of me. I was quite put off by it all and decided to pick a fight by asking him a question: "Babe, how come when I'm looking good, you don't even turn your head and acknowledge me, but when I'm a mess like this, you can't keep your hands off of me?" I thought I had him good on this one, but instead, he stepped back, put his hand on his chin and took a moment to respond. He broke the silence and said, "I guess that's because you give that part of yourself away to everyone else, but I'm the only one who gets this part of you." Wow! I was not expecting that, and let's just say I was no longer annoyed and welcomed the once-rejected advances.

The point being, God wants you, *all of you*, messy bun and everything else that comes with you. He doesn't care about what you want others to see or what you cover up or filter. He wants you in your beautiful, chaotic mess. He fully knows you and fully loves you, and that's saying something right there.

Here's a question worth asking: If God wants us and sees value in us, why do we keep going back to that past view of ourselves? Because we dress ourselves in shame. Shame is relational in nature, expressing itself as our identity.[1] In contrast, guilt is more of a judicial word imploring us to believe we've done something erroneous.[2] Think back to when you were a kid and you did something you weren't supposed to. Did you perceive that you made a mistake and paid a consequence, or did you discern from the situation that you were bad and you continually replayed the event in your mind?

If you experienced the latter, then you have felt the pain of shame.

Even after choosing Christ as my Lord and serving in the church, I often found myself dressed in layers of shame, seeing a reflection of what was, not what is or what is to come. We can still often see that girl in the mirror . . . you know, the one we don't like. The one who made all the mistakes. The one who was abused. The one who was made fun of. The one who fell into stereotypes. The one who had a bad reputation. The one who let everyone down. The one who was rejected. The one that can't break the cycle. Shame refuses to let us move forward, making us want to hide.

When I was a kid, my mom would play a cruel, but funny, joke on our friends that would come over to our house for the first time. She would innocently say, "Let's play a game!" Then proceed to get out a blanket and throw it over our guests and tell them to take off one thing they didn't need. They would always start with something small like a watch or a shoe, and she would, article after article, repeat, "That's not it." Once they began to take their socks off, she would quickly end the game before it progressed; meanwhile, we were all laughing that not once did they think to take the blanket off!

Shame keeps us hiding underneath that blanket, working tirelessly to shed any resemblance of our past but never allowing ourselves to come fully into the light. We hinge our thoughts about ourselves and acceptance by our community on these "if only" statements, keeping us from living an authentic life:

- ♥ If they only knew what I used to do for a living.
- ♥ If they only knew the thoughts that I battle with.
- ♥ If they only knew what my home life was like.
- ♥ If they only knew I had an affair.
- ♥ If they only knew I had an abortion.
- ♥ If they only knew my sexual history.
- ♥ If they only knew my secret addictions.

The list could go on and on, and we find ourselves being smothered to death with thoughts that suck the life out of us.

So how do we take the blanket off? I will tell you how it happened for me. It wasn't planned, and it wasn't even intentional on my part, but it was totally, brutally, beautifully honest. I was in the car running some errands with a friend when she asked me to share my testimony with her. To be honest, I never thought I had a testimony. I am a preacher's kid and knew what was right and still chose to do what was wrong. "I don't have a testimony," I would tell myself. "All I have is mistakes, and I am one of them." These are the thoughts that tormented me continuously.

Nonetheless, that particular day I found myself sharing the good, the bad and the ugly things I had only ever hid under that blanket. I cried and I ugly cried in that car. In that moment, I released all of the shame that had been weighing me down. I felt a physical, spiritual and mental weight come off me! I immediately felt ten pounds lighter.

Therefore, confess your sins to one another
and pray for one another, that you may be healed . . .
James 5:16 (NIV)

We often work so hard to cover things up because our worldview tells us that once exposed, we will lose. We will lose relationships, we will lose influence, we will lose reputation. However, a biblical view tells us to expose our sins, and in doing so, we will be healed. In my own experience, I've found that in healthy relationships, we actually become more intimate when we share and expose our mess to each other.

My husband and I go to occasional checkups with our counselor to help us when we are stuck and to help us see things we couldn't on our own. During a session, the counselor told my husband that he needed to share some recent hurts with me. I knew he was going through some big things, but he was shutting me out. It was painful to watch him and not be able to help him, but he would not allow me to enter the pain with him. I ached because he ached, but the lack of sharing was actually pushing us away from each other.

After that guidance, he began to share his heartbreak and disappointments with me. It drew us closer to each other and gave him a safe place for processing and healing. The counselor told him that when men share their feelings with women, it's like honey to bees! It really is.

Be Whole

Let's go back to the bronze mirrors that we talked about at the beginning of this chapter. These mirrors were melted and remolded to become one large bronze laver, which is just a fancy word for a cup. This laver was a massive basin that would hold water, which scripturally is a symbol of the Holy Spirit (John 7:37-39). The priest would come to these lavers and use the water in them to cleanse their hands and feet before going into the most sacred part of the tabernacle, called the holy of holies, to symbolize the removal of anything unclean, signifying purity (Exodus 30:19).

Do you know what this means? When we willingly bring our past, dim views of ourselves to God, He redeems us! He then brings our collective stories together as the body of Christ and crafts us into a useful vessel of honor. He deems each of us as worthy vessels to be filled with the Holy Spirit, and He uses our stories to bring others directly into His presence!

So as you look in the mirror today, I challenge you to not see the flaws and worn-out labels or to hate this girl who is way more than the sum total of her mistakes. God, your Father, is grieved by any loss of relationship and wants to restore your sight to His original design. Take a closer look into the story of your life and celebrate the freedom and future that's already been bought and paid for. Take an inventory of critical words that should no longer hold you hostage. Be open with others and take that blanket of shame off. *Be whole.*

"God will not look you
over for medals, degrees or
diplomas, but for scars."
-Elbert Hubbard

The simple believe anything,
but the prudent give
thought to their steps.
Proverbs 14:15 (NIV)

Chapter 2
Be Smart

We've all been fooled a time or two in our lives, but in the famous words of George W. Bush, "Fool me once, shame on you. Fool me—can't get fooled again!" When I was little, my mom had fooled me when she repeatedly said that she had eyes in the back of her head, and I would marvel. When she was napping one day, I got brave enough to part her long, dark hair and discovered there were no additional eyes keeping watch on me! Oh, the freedom I felt!

It is important to investigate the words spoken to us, whether internally or externally. Be smart. It's time to reflect on perceptions about yourself and others that you embraced without first exploring their origination and validity. We've all experienced defining moments throughout our lives that have shaped us—whether for the good or for the bad. We don't always think about them, but they often show themselves through the way we respond to life. They become a filter through which we hear things and view things and can become our ceiling or our floor.

In talking with a counselor, I began to expose some of these moments, especially during a particular exercise he made me do. For homework, he asked me to write down my most painful memories. The task was completely daunting. I thought, "Where do I even begin?" My life, at that point, seemed like a big ball of hurt, and I couldn't find the ends to even start to untangle the mess. Sitting down, staring at a blank Word document with the cursor blinking, begging me to say something, I reluctantly visited my thirteen-year-old self.

Going Back

We often have to go back to our childhood. I'm a firm believer that the enemy comes in at an early age to seed thoughts that will cripple our view of ourselves and others, thoughts intended to delay or even completely derail our God-sized dreams. Think about it: Do you still have a voice ringing in your ear? A teacher? Your mom? Your dad? A boss? Kids from school? Just before you go up for a promotion, as you get ready for a date, make a purchase, put on a swimsuit, what thoughts or experiences run through your head? When was the moment your confidence was shaken or even stolen?

For me, it happened in middle school. Middle school can wreak havoc on any adolescent, and it certainly didn't spare me. Going back to visit those years uncovered some dreadful moments. I was homeschooled, but my sixth- and seventh-grade years were especially challenging educationally as well as emotionally. We moved to a new state, in a small town, where my dad took over an old church as the senior pastor. The move was hard in every way. We went from having a vibrant community of homeschool friends to being the only homeschool family in the town. We left our best friends, a church we loved and everything that made us feel comfortable and secure.

Although our next two years accomplished so much for the kingdom, with the many outreaches and ministries my parents started, for me, they were also filled with many tears and lonely times. To be truthful, so much was going on at the church, I often felt unnoticed. Today my dad incessantly reminds me to not miss out on my kids the way he felt he missed out on us because of the demands of ministry and misplaced priorities. I'm grateful for his continuous reminders, especially in busy seasons. I often hear his voice ringing in my ears, challenging me to see my family and make them my first ministry.

The busyness of building a church, coupled with the fact that my mom faced many health challenges over those middle school years, left me to do things on my own. My education fell behind, especially in English. Up to this point, I had always done well in school, making As and Bs, so getting my first of many Cs was embarrassing. It seeded a thought in me that I wasn't smart, especially compared to my straight-A older sister. Comparison is such a thief! I wish that unhealthy seed had been choked out, but instead, I kept skirting by unnoticed with everything else going on at home, and the small seed grew into the largest weed of my adolescence.

After two years, we moved back to what we deemed "the Promised Land," the great country of Texas. By this point my sisters and I were begging my parents to put us in a school because we were desperate to have friends again. I was so excited and nervous all at the same time to enter my new school and my first "real" school as an eighth grader! Do you remember those butterfly moments just before school would start? I'm sure my mom had a few butterflies of her own sending her kids to school for the first time, and she certainly didn't want to send us unprepared.

My loving mother began to notice how far behind I was in English, so in an effort to prepare me for school, she ordered the popular *Hooked On Phonics* program, which helped beginner readers learn to read through the use of phonics. If you were around in the early 90s, you'll remember the commercials well: "Hooked on phonics worked for me!" And you may also remember the many late-night comedy shows mocking it—they certainly grabbed my ear.

I sat on the couch with my mom as she made me do the lessons with my younger sister, who was seven years old at the time. As if I wasn't embarrassed enough to do the lessons to begin with, now I felt even more humiliated to be put on the same level as a first grader. Together we were prompted to sound out words and repeat . . . "ch-," "sh-," "th-," "qu-."

What thirteen-year-old needs help being insecure? I felt very, very small. I was hurt, embarrassed, and from that moment on, I disqualified myself from so many things. I knew one thing for sure, I was not smart. As a result, I didn't raise my hand in school, I sat at the back of the classroom as often as possible, I didn't make eye contact with the teacher to hopefully keep from getting called on, I didn't apply to any college, I never wanted to read or speak in front of people . . . the list goes on and on. It was demoralizing.

Setup

Joshua had his own journey with learning how to be smart. Enslaved in Egypt from birth to around forty years old, I can imagine he had some demoralizing moments as well. His whole life he had been told what he could and couldn't do, where he could and couldn't go and confined by his ability to labor excessively hard for another man's profit. He was a slave, his dad was a slave, and for four hundred years, that's all he could see in his family line. Then the God that he had prayed to, heard stories about and worshipped miraculously shows up and sets all of Israel free. But how do you truly live free when you've only ever known enslavement?

True freedom can only come from the one that has authored freedom for us. Not only does God have the power to set us free, but He knows, in full detail, how He has specifically wired you and designed you for greatness. The challenge comes in the rewiring of our thoughts after so long of being told things that are contrary to God's original design for us. Joshua came from the strongest clan of Israel, Ephraim, so he was no stranger to hard labor (Numbers 13:8), but God did not give him strength to build another man's empire. Joshua had a bigger purpose that the Lord would rewire in his

39

thinking. He wasn't built to be a slave, he was built to be a warrior.

The enemy did not want Joshua to know that he had strength to be a warrior. Similarly, the very things that God gifted me with were the very things the enemy would work to discredit and oppress in my life. I remember my senior year working diligently in my English class on a paper that would be a massive part of my grade for the year. I usually didn't try hard so I wouldn't feel disappointed in my inability, but this time, I gave it my all. I got up the courage to let my dad read my paper and asked for his feedback. I hung my head in disappointment as he told me it was just "OK." Without much expectation, I handed in my paper to my teacher, but when I received it back, I saw it was more than OK. I didn't just get an A, my teacher said that it was so well written she wanted my permission to use it as an example to the rest of her classes! The enemy didn't want me to know that I had the gift of words to deliver hope to others.

For goodness sakes, you are reading a book written by a girl who struggled to read! Over the years I've ministered on many platforms, on multiple continents to thousands of people; led and inspired hundreds of volunteers; guest-blogged for many ministries and sat at tables to glean from some of the most brilliant minds, things I never thought possible for someone as insignificant as myself. If I can tell you something today that I hope will stay with you, it would be to *be smart!* Be smart and discern when you are being deceived by the enemy. Don't fall for his tricks.

*So that we would not be outwitted by Satan:
for we are not ignorant of his designs.*
2 Corinthians 2:11 (ESV)

Think back . . . do you remember a time in your early years that made a significant mark on you? Were you humiliated? Laughed at? Passed over? Abandoned? Let's look at these moments from a twenty-thousand-foot view. You were just a kid, and yet you were hit by hurts that you didn't know how to handle. These hurts may still impact you today. Why? Because the enemy wants to put dysfunction around your destiny!

The enemy wants to put dysfunction around your destiny!

Where has the enemy worked to outwit you? Some of our greatest trials, hurts and hang-ups came from schemes to keep us from reaching our greatest potential. Don't fall for it. *Be Smart.*

The enemy knew the potential that I had in the fabric of my being, just like he knows that God made you and wired you for greatness. So *why* do we so often operate like we are still thirteen? Why do we not challenge ourselves to push past false limitations that the enemy has intimidated us with since we were kids, much like the boogie man in the closet? As an adult, I know that my intelligence is not based on how well I read at thirteen, yet I kept this filter of myself and allowed it to cloud my view for a good majority of my life.

I can now see how the enemy wanted me to keep those thoughts and insecurities buried deep inside of me, so he could be the only one to nurture them.

Needless to say, the homework from my counselor stunk. I had to humble myself to say these events in my life actually hurt me and I had allowed them to define me and hold me captive for years and years. I allowed it by ignoring it. I allowed it because of pride. I allowed it because it was easier than dealing with it. Now, I had to choose to challenge the dysfunction in my head that had been choking out my potential for far too long!

It chokes us for a long time because as we age, instead of embracing wisdom, our pride begins to blossom and tells us that we can handle things on our own. What twenty-, thirty-, forty-, or fifty-plus-year-old wants to admit that their "issues" in life were from a childhood incident, a name they were called, or a bully who wouldn't let up? It feels embarrassing that we've clung to it for so long, so we ignore it.

May I ask you, what is it that you are still holding on to? What triggers drudge up voices that you thought were buried and gone? Do you still hold the same labels over yourself: dumb, fat, stupid, failure, rebellious, bad, dirty, disappointment? Whatever it is, I encourage you to write it down, locate its origin and be brave enough to share it with a trusted friend or counselor. Acknowledge the pain of it and choose to uproot the wrong thinking that's been nurtured by you. It's time to be done once and for all! It's time to be smart by facing this head-on and moving past false limitations. You have so much more in you that is begging for a chance to shine. Let's break the dysfunction. Let's break the constant chatter in your head. Let's break off what is breaking you!

Stepping Out

The Lord sent Moses to Egypt to set Israel free, but Joshua and all of the rest of the people still had to choose to follow him. As Joshua stood at the banks of the Red Sea, with Pharaoh's army in hot pursuit, I wonder what thoughts ran through his head. Right before his eyes the Lord parted the waters, and Joshua went for it, stepping out into the unknown and away from everything that limited him. His eyes were opened to dream and create a life that once seemed impossible.

He knew this for sure: God could and would do anything! Imagine being a slave all those years, then suddenly having the hope of a future and a blank slate to become whoever you want to be! By accepting Jesus Christ as our Lord and Savior, we too can experience a blank-slate moment to become who He has always meant for us to be. God can and will do miraculous things in your life if you choose to step out of an enslaved mindset and step into the impossible. We've all been a slave to some outlandish thoughts, but it's time to live free!

Miracles follow obedience, movement, testing and much discomfort.

Although the Israelites experienced many miracles from plagues to parting seas, they were produced through faith, personal sacrifice and hard work. Miracles follow obedience, movement, testing and much

43

discomfort. Freedom is never free. There is always a cost we have to be willing to pay.

Joshua's first assignment recorded in scripture was to lead Israel into battle. Talk about going for greatness—from slave to warrior! He didn't allow the past or systemic bondage to keep him from being fooled out of his God-given purpose or identity. No, he stood up and led them into battle.

I too had to go from slave to warrior in my mindset. I had been enslaved by my thoughts concerning myself and the shortcomings I possessed. I distinctly remember my college speech class. I avoided it until I absolutely had to take it. Every speech I gave I was *miserable*. No matter how well written my speech was, I had about sixty seconds before I felt the heat begin rising from my feet all the way through my face. Tomato red, I would then begin to shake so violently that it was hard to speak and even harder to walk back to my seat. My knees knocked so fiercely, I could barely sit down when it was all over. It was painful . . . It was painful for everyone in the room! I made an inner vow that I would never speak in public. I got my grade and washed my hands of it.

Years later, I had been praying to the Lord about a deeper level of obedience and trust. I had made another oath with the Lord that I would walk through every door that He opened up for me. I didn't know what He would ask me to do when I made that oath, or it may have come with a few addendums. Not long after that, I received a call from a small church, who was hosting a women's event, and they asked if I would come and minister as their guest speaker. I was mortified, and I was about to give a polite "No, I'm so busy right now and here's a list of much more qualified people to do that" response when the Lord reminded me of my oath of obedience. Our pain from the past can become a place of disobedience if we excuse ourselves from doing what God has asked us to do.

> *Our pain from the past can become a place of disobedience if we excuse ourselves from doing what God has asked us to do.*

I cried. I sat in my car, like I had just received a death sentence, and uncontrollably wept. I prayed, "Lord, if women can miraculously receive salvation through my red neck and shaking hands, then I am willing to be a fool for you." I had no expectation that my experience would be different from my college speech class, but I just thought that maybe somehow God could couple my inability with His presence to bring salvation to the room.

For three months I prepared for this message. I wrote it, preached it in a mirror, cried about it, prayed about it, called it stupid, tore it up, started over, doubted and yet still showed up that night for the battle, I mean event. I told my pastor, who had committed to pray for me, "If someone doesn't get saved from this, it's not worth it."

I stood alone in the pastor's office of that small church the night of the event. I worshiped. I cried. I surrendered and I declared. I walked out of his office the tallest five-foot-three I've ever been! My confidence had grown considerably in that short time of prayer, but with every step toward the auditorium, I got smaller and smaller. My thoughts wandered as I rehearsed what would happen to me just sixty seconds into speech class.

My husband was ministering through worship that night, and right before we started, I walked up to him as he put on his guitar strap and said in a very soft, shaky voice, "I don't think I can do this." I wanted to cry . . . again. He looked at me and very strongly said, "Yes you can. Now get back to your seat." I said, "OK." I hung my head low and headed back to my seat.

I couldn't get out of it. I was stuck, and now this room of fifty women felt like two million people surrounding me with expectations I didn't think I could deliver. Maybe this is why I identify so much with Joshua who stepped into battle for the first time, not as an experienced warrior, but through a spirit of obedience. The only escape I could see was worship. I made my altar on the front row that night and pushed aside all my fear, threw my hands up and gave Jesus my all. I knew I had to step into the water like Moses did in the parting of the Red Sea as they left their life of slavery behind, but I was determined to not go into the deep alone.

Victory is won through obedience, not experience.

After worship they introduced me and nothing had changed, the butterflies were swarming, but the moment I got out of my seat, with each step to the pulpit, I felt power, poise and strength come over me. I did not shake. I did not stutter. I did not turn red. I delivered the message the Lord had penned through my obedience, and three women gave their lives to Christ that night. I will never forget those three.

Higher Ground

My pastor from home immediately connected with me after the event to see if anyone had responded to the call for salvation. She had been on a higher ground, a different vantage point interceding for victory. She rejoiced with me, not in what I did but in the lives that were eternally changed. In the weeks that came after that night, I asked God, "Why was my experience that night so different from my experience in speech class?" He impressed this on my heart, "I want you to see that *with* me, what you couldn't do *without* me is possible." The reverent fear of God entered me that day to a level I will never forget. Without

What you couldn't do without God is possible with God.

God, I'm a shaky, insecure, red mess, but with God, I am a mighty warrior, even if the shakes occasionally creep in!

It's equally important to realize that the devil is a liar and a good one at that. I am not a dumb girl marked with ignorance and destined for the ordinary. I am marked by God, and now unstoppable for His purposes and glory. Be smart. You are not who you've thought you were!

If the enemy can't cripple us with insecurity, he will certainly work to fill us with pride.

The only way we can truly be smart is to know that God is with us and to fully understand that everything that is good in us or successful through us is because of God. If the enemy can't cripple us with insecurity, he will certainly work to fill us with pride.

When we are filled with pride, we are not smart enough to see the bigger picture, which is detrimental to the battles we will face and the victories we will steward. Israel didn't pick a fight, the fight came to them. The Amalekites attacked, and they responded. Moses, Israel's leader, appointed Joshua to lead the newly formed army and told him that while he was fighting, he would be standing on the top of the hill with the staff that God gave him in his hands (Exodus 17:9). This is an important notation for us because sometimes, in the battles we face, all we see is the enemy that is pressing toward us and we don't realize that God has set people on higher ground to fight for us. They are still in it with you, and though you may not be able to see or hear them in your battle, their role in your victory is bigger than you can imagine.

After Joshua had won the victory with the sword, God gave Moses some very clear instructions: "*Write this on a scroll as something to be remembered AND make sure that Joshua hears it . . .*" (Exodus 17:14 NIV). There's a partnership between the physical swords and the spiritual swords that we are armed with and carry in times of battle. I can go to a counselor and do all of his steps, but without the partnership with the Holy Spirit my efforts are going to be futile. It's the power of the Holy Spirit that gives us the ability to truly change from the inside out.

Yes, Joshua was given the victory on the battle ground, but God wanted him to see you're not all that, for it is God who wins the victory. You are a part, not the whole. Moses was on top of that hill, and each time he lifted the rod the Lord had given him, Joshua would advance, but each time he got tired and lowered his arms, Joshua would falter. In addition, if it hadn't been for Aaron and Hur seeing the weight Moses was carrying and coming up underneath his arms to give him the added support he needed, Joshua's fate would not have looked the same.

Moses didn't send reports to the battlefield of what was happening from higher ground; instead, he focused on the spiritual and supernatural parts of the battle. Some would say that he wasn't getting his hands dirty on the battlefield and, therefore, wasn't doing anything of value; others will see that he did all the heavy lifting.

At the beginning of 2022, I got hit with COVID-19. I was so upset at the timing of it all because during this particular week of January my church has a time of prayer and fasting together that I look forward to. Each night of the week we meet, pray and worship, believing God will do big things throughout the year. During night one of these meetings I had a choice to make: Was I going to stay in my bed and give in to sickness or was I going to get up and fight? I chose to fight! I got out of my bed, even on nights where it was begging me to stay, and joined my church via live stream. Quarantine couldn't keep me quiet! I worshiped for an audience of one every single night that week. I had a beautiful, intimate time with the Lord even in my sickness. I was all by myself, but yet felt encouraged, full of faith, and I received my healing.

After I recovered, I went to church and a leader came up to me and began to share a dream that she had. She said that on Monday night she dreamed that I was standing by myself worshiping. In her dream, she came up behind me, laid her hands on my shoulders and began to pray. When she woke up, she didn't know what I was going through and didn't feel led to call me. She felt led to pray for me. Little did she know that the very night she had the dream was the night I got my positive COVID test and stood privately worshiping God behind closed doors. I was by myself, thinking I was all alone, but I was not alone in the battle. I didn't overcome alone, even though there were times I felt lonely. What I couldn't see in the natural was occurring in the supernatural, not because of me, but because of those God had called to fight for me.

Maybe you feel like no one is fighting for you. I understand your struggle, but the truth is we are never alone. One night as I was tucking my daughter, Kya, into bed, we began to pray as we always do. After I was done, she took a turn, and at only nine years old, she began to pray over a specific child that had lost both their mother and father. She did not know their name, but with intention, she began to speak God's provision and protection over this boy that God put in her heart. She will likely never know him on this side of eternity, but she will on the next. No matter your life experience, you are seen by God and you can be sure your family in the body of Christ is praying for you. Be strengthened and encouraged today, for there is someone on higher ground with their focus on your victory.

God gets the glory

So you're in the middle of facing a real enemy like Joshua did. It's tangible. There are things coming at you right and left:

daggers, swords and flaming arrows that seem to be aimed right at the heart. From diagnosis to disease, financial disaster, devastating relational heartache and loss that feels unbearable, the attack is relentless. At points in the battle, you feel like you are taking one step forward, receiving a breakthrough or making some type of improvement, only to then be hit and be pushed two steps back. In addition, no one is calling you or texting you the encouragements you feel you need. This is exactly what was happening to Joshua when he was on the battlefield.

I can imagine the confusion he may have felt mid-battle. He was just being obedient, doing what he was asked to do, and for no apparent reason, he was winning, losing, winning, losing like a yo-yo being played with. If it had been me, I know I would have struggled with thoughts of inadequacy and questioned if I was actually made for more. I still battle those thoughts from time to time, wanting to retreat to critical words spoken over me and the small view of myself the enemy authors for me. Maybe in the middle of your battle, you too feel like some cruel universal joke is being played on you, and you don't know if God is in it with you. Stay strong, my friend. The story is not over!

All of a sudden, Joshua felt this power and determination come over him, and he pushed through with his sword and led his men to victory. I am declaring over you today that the power of God is going to come over you and lead you to victory! God is on your side, and so am I. I can imagine the fist bumps that started happening at that moment for the army of Israel. For four hundred years they had to endure pain and oppression, but this day they faced a real bully and slew it with a sword!

It's easy in victory to bask in the glory of the battlefield, but we often miss our responsibility in our victories. Moses, who was unseen and possibly from some vantage points seemed uninvolved, didn't post a selfie or throw a big party; he built an altar and he named it "For the Lord is my banner." Too many times, we take the credit as if our tragedy-to-triumph stories were won by our own hands.

Even in my own journey, I could ignore the major accomplishments of my mother who went to war for me time and time again. As a child I could only see my deficiencies and the accusations the enemy was hurling at me, but my mom was on the mountain top, unstoppable in her resolve to see me move forward in education, my spiritual development and successes. Yes, in my lifetime I have done great things, not because of my own gifts or power but because of God, who sits on the throne, and my mother, who stood on the mountain top unseen.

For our struggle is not against flesh and blood,
but against the rulers, against the authorities,
against the powers of this dark world and against
the spiritual forces of evil in the heavenly realms.
Ephesians 6:12 (NIV)

The battles we face are first defeated in realms we cannot quantify and sometimes we need a reminder of the reality of spiritual warfare in our self-made culture. Let's not allow the world to seep pride into our God-breathed victories. Even now, each time the Lord asks me to share on any platform, I pray, "God let them see you and not me." I want to reflect the glory of God and when praise comes to me for what God has done, I want to deflect the praise right back to Him!

Builder

Just like Joshua, in my life, I've had to press forward to build the woman I wanted to become. By my late twenties I had never read a book, except for the Bible. I somehow made it through school with CliffsNotes and friends sharing their readings with me so I could pass tests and quizzes and write papers. I honestly didn't think I could read well enough to comprehend, so I didn't try, but as an adult I chose to not stay in that defeated mentality. With the revelations my counselor helped uncover through the exercises shared, I began to work on changing my thought life to end the needless cruelty in my mind and to push myself to be more and do more.

I began to stand up against the voices that used to make decisions for me. That looked like putting scriptures on my mirrors to speak God's Word over myself so I could see what He sees. When fear would try to tell me I couldn't do something, I instead let that drive me to try even more. When I felt intimidated by others, instead of comparing myself to them, I let their abilities be a teacher to me, creating a gratitude instead of a negative attitude. By being brave enough to do these things, I was enlightened and freed to read, learn and grow. I discovered that by humbly acknowledging what happened and the hurts it produced, it was no longer a confidence breaker; instead, it became a confidence builder! I discovered I wasn't who I thought I was all those years. My "I can't(s)" turned into "I can(s)," and it gave me the energy to explore new spaces and passions.

What tried to break confidence can instead build confidence!

Once you have gained the wisdom and have been smart enough to recognize the way Satan deceived you, you need to be smart enough to use that wisdom to in turn build up others. In my exciting new space of awareness, I also had some hurtful revelations. In an effort to hide my embarrassing inadequacies, I unknowingly hurt people because I was trying to control and protect my image. It's painful for me to look back at my life and see the catastrophe of people that I unintentionally impacted negatively because I didn't want them to think I was as stupid as I felt. Of course, staying in that kind of regret will get us nowhere, so instead I have chosen to become a builder.

The wise woman builds her house, but with her own hands the foolish one tears hers down.
Proverbs 14:1 (NIV)

As wise women, we can release people to win because we don't have to be in control. We can encourage others by sharing the things that once held us back because we aren't defined by our losses. We can build people up because we aren't concerned that it might affect our own status. We can bring other people along in our successes because we don't need the credit. I don't know about you, but I want to be a builder of myself and others.

Now, I can easily identify those who are walking in brokenness because I lived it. I see it in their eyes, in their false confidence trying to project authority, yet longing for validation. I see it through their fear-based decisions that holds them back and others too. I see it in their lack of authentic, transparent relationships. However, I can do more than see it. I can take the confidence I have through my healing in Christ and weaponize it to break off what is breaking others! That is my hope for this book, that you, as my friend and reader, experience freedom from the weight of brokenness. God is not trying to break you, He wants to build you and in turn you will build others.

Wherever you find yourself today, you are a part, not the whole. It's not all on you or all about you. God has connected you with men and women who will have a different vantage point; honor that. Recognize the tactics of the enemy, whether he uses the voice of insecurity from past experiences or the voice of accusation against those you couldn't see in the midst of your battle. Investigate the words that have kept you enslaved and push past those limiting spaces because you have so much more in you that is begging for a chance to shine. Be brave enough to say to the Lord, "I'll do it even if I look like a fool." Remember that God has made you for greatness; you don't need to prove anything to anyone, just rely on the Holy Spirit to guide your way. Never forget you were not, are not and will not be alone! It's time to *be smart.*

"Relationships move at
the speed of trust."
-Stephen M.R. Covey

If a house is divided against itself,
that house cannot stand.
Mark 3:25 (NIV)

Chapter 3
Be Trustworthy

I'm a sucker for survival shows! I don't know what it is that keeps me binge-watching them on streaming sites. I hate camping and have never been hunting, but it blows my mind watching how people can survive some of the most brutal environments with such limited resources! I don't know how people can willingly put themselves in circumstances that are without a doubt going to bring them pain.

What amazes me even more is that most of the time it's the relational struggles, not the environmental ones, that cause a group member to tap out of the challenge. They can handle no food, bugs, getting soaked with rain, spiders, snakes, ticks, but they can't handle their differences, hard conversations, or rejection.

Maybe that's what I identify with. The fact that I can handle the hard work, no sleep and more month than money, but if

I'm being honest, it's hard for me to handle the pain of rejection. Being a preacher's kid, I've experienced a lot of relational wounding from church members who were with us one minute and out the next, making it hard to truly trust people. As a result, my friend groups have been small, but once we are friends, I am loyal to a fault. I remember a particularly difficult season of rejection that almost broke me.

I had friends that I enjoyed; I was getting ready to have baby number three, which had been such a great pregnancy; and I had decided I was going to leave my job and stay at home and just soak up some good mommy moments. I had no idea that my world was about to get flipped upside down. Have you ever felt on top of the world, and then in what seemed like a flash, everything came crashing down?

In a six-month time period, I had a baby, went through postpartum and found out my close-knit friends were actually not friends to me at all. I thought I could trust them with everything, but instead, I went from having welcomed unannounced visits and always making extra food for whoever might drop by at dinner time to having no one to call to share good or bad news with. The pain was so deep, but I didn't know how to process it or if I even had the courage to face it. We often want to brush our pain under a metaphoric rug and just get on with it. In a day where "women rule the world," we put on masks and get really good at fixing surface-level imperfections, all while ignoring the ticking time bombs inside of us that are a moment away from exploding.

I wanted to hide, but the only place I could was in plain sight. So I hid my pain under a well-maintained face of makeup and pretended my way through my responsibilities. I "put my big girl panties on" and wouldn't let anyone see the vital organs that were tragically damaged and shutting down. I quickly wrapped up my stay-at-home-mom season and said yes to a position that I thought would restore my brokenness and prove my worth, but boy was I wrong.

The team was less than happy, to say the least, that I was coming on board to take over. Some of them were ten, twenty, thirty years my senior, and to be fair, the rollout was more like a crash landing, and I was definitely underqualified and overexposed. Every day I was met with more and more problems and my emotional weight made my 110-pound body feel like a 1,000-pound anchor. I couldn't keep going, but I was taught to never quit, press through, get up and get over it. So that's just what I did: I drove and I drove hard. The problem is that if you can't stop crying, you should probably let someone else into the driver's seat, at least long enough for you to be able to see clearly again. It's OK to realize you need to pull over in seasons for rest and healing.

We grieve to the level that we loved, so when trust is broken in relationships, we need appropriate space for healing. None of which I gave myself.

One day at work I barely held it together long enough to get through a meeting and to the bathroom before the waterworks came uncontrollably. I don't remember what was said. I don't remember who was there. All I remember is the continued feeling of rejection that I couldn't escape. I self-coached, fixed my makeup, took a deep breath, staged a smile and straightened up my posture to move on with the next meeting.

I made it through that day, but the issue was as soon as the sun set, it would rise again. I'd hoped that I would wake up and that "time would heal" my broken heart, but time just added more layers of complexity as I tried to ignore unresolved disappointment.

Finally, one night at home, I looked at my husband and I got up enough courage to say in desperation, "Babe, I'm not doing well." He didn't know what to say. Finally, he responded, "But you are so strong." I've always been the kind of woman that wanted a sword, not a tiara, but this time my sword was honesty. I told him, "I'm not doing well emotionally, and I can't keep this up anymore. I need help." I didn't realize it at that moment, but I had a revelation: time does not heal, but help can.

Time does not heal, but help can.

> *I lift up my eyes to the hills.*
> *From where does my help come?*
> *My help comes from the LORD,*
> *the Maker of heaven and earth.*
> *He will not allow your foot to slip;*
> *your Protector will not slumber.*
> *Psalm 121:1-3 (NIV)*

That desperate moment of vulnerability led to a new type of fight in me. I wasn't going to keep steamrolling past my past or over the poor people that were tragically in my pathway; I was finally going to face it. ALL of it. My loving husband encouraged me to do whatever I needed. I vowed to God that my focus over the next year would be healing for my soul. I was determined to receive my healing fully, and I wouldn't stop seeking the help I needed until I found it.

I realized that my emotional, spiritual and mental health was in my hands. No one could make the decision to be healed for me. I had to not only desire healing for myself but be willing to seek it out. Christ paid for every healing I would ever need on the cross, but it was my responsibility to ask for it, seek it out and knock until I fully received it for myself.

Relational Alarms

I wonder how many of us have found ourselves ready and willing to tap out of God's plan for our lives because of the relational and emotional tensions and pains we have experienced. Are you ready to give up on your promise because you couldn't have a hard conversation? Because you were hurt? Because you couldn't let it go and forgive? Or because it is hard for you to lay down your pride and say, "I'm sorry"? Possibly, you weren't willing to do the hard work of healing after betrayal. Whatever the case, I hope you have enough courage to keep reading.

Joshua also endured relational pains that could have easily taken him off course. He was chosen for another mission that was important and adventurous in nature. I'm sure it started off with excitement, but we'll soon see how it ended:

*The Lord said to Moses, "Send some men to explore the
land of Canaan, which I am giving to the Israelites. From
each ancestral tribe send one of its leaders." Numbers 13:1-2
(NIV)*

Joshua was one of the twelve selected to explore the land
promised to Israel. It wasn't a quick or easy trip, but it was one
that would change the trajectory of their lives forever. It is
estimated that they had to journey five hundred miles together
on this adventure.³ Can you imagine? That's an average of
twelve and a half miles per day, and they had no vehicle or
running shoes to make their travel comfortable! So off they
went on their forty-day survival challenge!

Not much is said about what happened between the time they
left and the time they returned. All we know is that at the end
of their forty-day adventure together, exploring the land, the
group came back and gave a report to the whole community.
The team shared how they had found milk, honey and all the
fruit they could dream of (all good and positive here). Then,
the team began to share about how large and fortified the
cities were, and in front of everyone (millions of people in the
assembly), they started sharing about the "giants" they saw and
how they were itty-bitty compared to the men they observed.

The crowd was completely frightened, and I can only imagine
how stunned Joshua and his friend Caleb were at the reports
that were given by their fellow explorers. You'd think after five
hundred miles they'd be on the same page, able to rely upon
each other, principled in their account, but due to their
reckless words, fear spread like wildfire through all of Israel!
Joshua and Caleb tore their clothes in desperation to get the

people's attention. When they got it, they reminded them that the Lord was with them and that they could take the land, but instead of gaining the crowd back, the whole assembly turned on them and even talked about killing them. They went from being part of the elect twelve, chosen for a mission, to being target practice for friends turned haters! Talk about a violation of trust!

One group, twelve men and two different stories returned that day. These guys had spent the last forty days and five hundred miles together, yet something didn't add up. Sometimes we can grow up in the same home, but each member of the family relives stories from such a different perspective. The same family trip that brought you joy may have been a source of pain for someone else; there's a story behind the story that's begging to be told. What happened? Was there a disagreement? An offense? For forty days, the twelve spies had foraged together for their meals, been away from their wives and families, lived off the land and made makeshift shelters. So what happened to bring such division in their accounts? I wonder if there was a battle of who was going to be the alpha male. After all, Joshua and Caleb's first instinct to win over a crowd was to rip their shirts off!

Moses appointed twelve trusted representatives from each tribe; however, scripture doesn't indicate that Mosses assigned a leader to the group. The group was supposed to work together—in unity. Somehow this mission got diverted. It shifted from working together in order to find a route and strategy so they could move into this land to abandoning their promise, their call and their mission and taking as many people as they could down that path with them! Misery loves company, doesn't it?

I wonder if the division started small as they walked down unknown paths, "Who does he think he is?" "I think we should go this way." "I think we should sleep here." "I should be leading the way." "Why does he always get the credit?" Was there a misunderstanding? Was there jealousy? Could it have easily been dealt with if they had just talked it through? Or was it a heart issue? A faith issue? A trust issue?

Looking back at the betrayals I experienced, I can see distinct moments that should have set off alarms for me. For example, I wouldn't share about opportunities that came my way because I knew they would be met with jealousy instead of encouragement. In many conversations where offenses were shared, I'd challenge the thinking behind it. Many times, defending my leaders and setting a space of honor were not well received. I began to tiptoe around emotions to keep the peace, but what I should have noticed was how quiet I had become. I am an introvert by nature but get me alone and we will have deep conversations all day! Yet I couldn't be myself because I couldn't be honest. Trustworthy friends create safe places for you to be you.

Trustworthy friends create safe places for you to be you.

I love the scripture in Proverbs 27:17 that illustrates how friends are supposed to sharpen each other, like iron sharpening iron. I thought that's what I was doing when I would bring a different perspective, but instead of gaining strength from each other, I was impaled by dull daggers from behind that left deep wounds. In my efforts to sharpen, I discovered that people don't like to be challenged in their offense, in their place of comfort or in their direct disobedience to God. They don't always want to face the hard things or have the hard conversations. In my humanity, I desire to be around people who say what I want them to say. But just because someone in your life is making you "feel" better doesn't mean that they are making you better. Instead, you want friends that help you grow.

Just because someone in your life is making you "feel" better doesn't mean that they are making you better.

In addition, if you hold a place of influence, there will always be people who love your position but don't necessarily love you. I think most leaders can identify with the sentiment that leadership can be lonely. It's hurtful to find out that your genuine love and concern for someone is reciprocated with intentions to use your connections or resources and ultimately use you.

All of this should have been a red flag to me that there were deeper heart issues at play, but I just believed the best in people and gave them a full tank of trust. I didn't realize that I was setting myself up to be stranded on the side of the road. Here's an encouragement for you: boundaries are good and trust should be earned. Not that we walk around waiting to get hurt and always questioning people's motives, but we are instructed in the Word to guard our hearts in Psalm 104: 9. "You set a boundary they cannot cross."

Boundaries are a gift from God. They aren't meant to create walls to keep people out; they are meant to produce life-giving spaces for living waters, not overwhelming seas. People will only tell us what we let them, which means we can set the standard and expectations for our conversations. Guard your heart against deposits of division, know your worth and have wisdom to hear more than just what's being said.

Guard your heart against deposits of division.

Time and time again I've seen people get offended and disconnect from their local church because of someone else's offense! I sadly watch as their worlds fall apart because they easily gave ear to conversations that should have had godly boundaries around to protect their calling and character. So many of these offenses could have been cleared up in a matter of minutes, but instead, pride kept them from going to the person and vain imaginations created giants out of grasshoppers!

Let me ask you, are there people that you are avoiding? Not talking to? How many people are you smiling at, but in your head you're cursing at? You're giving them a holy hug, but you are choking them to death like a cartoon scene inside your head. Are you denying deeply rooted heart issues like jealousy, a religious spirit, offense or disappointment in order to not have confrontations that could expose what's really going on inside of you? I want you to hear this: relationships are so important to Christ. He wants you to be trustworthy. He wants you to be honest, be pure, be kind, be holy. He wants you to empty yourself of ambition, comparison and anything else that may keep you from your best. The enemy comes around prowling like a lion. He knows the promise God put in your heart and he wants you to see others as an obstacle to it. Why?

United we can do anything, but separated our impact is weak.

Because he knows that the united church is an unstoppable force! United we can do anything, but separated our impact is weak. This world needs a united church! It needs women who will confront the hard things, take correction and be on guard against offense.

Surrendering Control

Oftentimes we allow our disappointments or unmet expectations to cloud our judgement and separate us from the very thing that can bring us healing and life once again. As a response to deep, disheartening disappointments, we exchange trust for control. Control is such a cold, hard partner to live with. Have you ever worked for a controlling or overbearing boss that wouldn't let you breathe, think or create? It suffocates you.

We need to be bold enough to surrender control. We can feel unsteady when we do so. And often in times of trial, control rears its ugly head. After all, we think if we can know enough, our knowledge will help us think our way out of a situation, but that's contrary to scripture, which indicates that through Christ a spirit of peace will surpass our understanding, guarding our hearts and minds (Philippians 4:7). Have you ever fallen into the trap of control?

The voice of control sounds like this:

- ♥ Trust yourself and your knowledge.
- ♥ Micromanage every detail of your life and others'.
- ♥ It has to be done this way.
- ♥ If you're in charge, you won't fail.
- ♥ Assert power to get what you want.
- ♥ Hold all the details and make people reliant on you.
- ♥ Know everything that's going on in a person's life and become their permission giver.

Control inundates us with overthinking, relentlessly making us work hard to hold weights that are just too heavy for our humanity. Furthermore, it drives our relationships into rebellion because people are not puppets. We have to be bold and let it go—all of it!

Although my name means heavenly angel, my mom would often say to me that I was an angel in disguise because I was not exactly acting like an angel. It only takes me missing a meal or a night's sleep or being that time of the month for my thinking, perspective and attitude to be off. If that is true of me, why would I even consider trusting myself and trying to take control over my battles instead of trusting them in the hands of an infinite God who cannot go against His own name and has the power to change everything? I want my Provider, Healer, Banner, Peace, Shepherd, Righteous God who is faithful to be with me in it all to have *all* control!

You might be asking, "How do I hand over control when I am a control freak?" Listen, I like my towels folded a certain way too, so I get it. Relinquishing control starts with surrender. Over the years, I've surrendered titles, learning the hard lesson that money and position don't define me. I've surrendered my reputation, knowing that God would fight for me and that I could rest in Him. I've surrendered my future when things didn't go like I wanted them to, knowing that God's ways are higher than mine (Isaiah 55:9). I've surrendered my finances when I've made such a mess that they were only redeemable through God's economy. There are so many more situations I've tried to control over the years, but when I truly surrendered them to God, even when they couldn't be "fixed," I had peace that surpassed all my limited understanding around my circumstance.

Surrender came for me through confession.

> *Therefore confess your sins to each other and*
> *pray for each other so that you may be healed. The*
> *prayer of a righteous person is powerful and effective.*
> *James 5:16 (NIV)*

It's not that I like to confess. It's that I fear God enough to surrender when He opens my eyes to the error of my ways. At times, my heart was hard and angry. When we were a young married couple dealing with a sick baby and the medical debt that came steaming in as a result of it all, we were completely overwhelmed. We lived in a small apartment, barely able to get by. My husband was working for the church seven days a week, yet not even making minimum wage. I felt like no one cared about our situation, not even God.

Tithing was never an issue for me. Being raised in the church, I knew scripturally the first 10 percent was God's, and I didn't dare touch it. I trusted His Word and the calamity it would bring if I didn't return to God what was already His, but what about His promises to me? Where was He in this? It flipped a switch in me, and in my "I can take care of myself" attitude, I picked up two extra side jobs, in addition to my full-time job. It was obvious that our financial situation wasn't going to change unless I took control.

One year went by, and we were actually more in debt than when we started. Control had left me and our bank account more exhausted than ever. Daniel and I got into an argument about it all (financial issues are one of the main reasons for divorce by the way), and in the heat of things, he blurted out, "Do you ever think you are the reason we don't have any money?" In my flesh I had a one-two punch that would have knocked him out, but instead, the Holy Spirit gut punched me. We didn't talk the rest of the night, but I called him from work the next day. I asked him if he remembered what he said to me, and he profusely began to apologize, but I stopped him. I assured him I wasn't mad, because those weren't his words, they were the Holy Spirit's message to me. In all my striving, hurt, disappointment and anger, I hadn't trusted God to do what He does.

Everyone likes miracles, but no one ever wants to be in a position to need one. I swallowed my pride and surrendered my anger to God so He could take control. I quit all the extra stuff I was doing and just stayed faithful to what God had called me to. There was no knock on our door with a bag of cash or mail with a blank check, but God worked with me. He gave me strategies to work with the insurance companies and hospitals. He showed me how to save, meal plan and create a debt snowball.

Everyone likes miracles, but no one ever wants to be in a position to need one.

When we stayed committed to His plan and kept our ears tuned to what He was saying, the results were HGTV-makeover status. In one year's time we were completely out of debt, not just our medical debt, but also our credit cards, loans and cars were completely paid for. We both got promotions, and we not only gave our tithe but we also gave over and above our tithe with such joy and gratitude. The day I confessed and let go changed everything. The truth is we can't control anything, but we sure can hold up what God wants to do for us. Without God, I make a mess of things, but surrendering to God is supernatural every time.

Empty yourself of all the things that are keeping you from the presence of God because in His presence, all fear is gone. To top it all off, God holds no record of wrong, which means if you've surrendered something and then find yourself picking it back up, He won't get tired of you so bring it right back to Him!

Moving Forward

So what do you do when trust is broken? Joshua and Caleb felt the pain of betrayal, indicated by their shock given in the reports their comrades had given. They were grieved. The heartache of losing relationships is so deep, and they couldn't do anything in that moment to change their circumstance. The accusations that were hurled at them were deadly and for what? For just encouraging the people to be brave and do the right things? The rumors spread fast (I can relate), and they literally feared for their lives. You can do the right thing and still be done wrong, but you can be done wrong and still respond right. Don't let another person's decision corrupt your character. Do the hard work to heal.

> *You can do the right thing and still be done wrong, but you can be done wrong and still respond right.*

Healing is a choice. We can run from our hurts, but they just run alongside us. My husband often says, "Healing hurts, but not healing hurts too." You have to choose the hurt that's worth your focus. Healing will not just find you, you have to find it. When trust is violated, you may not be able to heal the relationship, but you can have a healed heart. God's Word will always give us a roadmap to healing. This is the path He sent me down to restore trust once again.

Ask and it will be given to you; seek and you will find; knock and the door will be opened to you. For everyone who asks receives; the one who seeks finds; and to the one who knocks, the door will be opened.
Matthew 7:7-8 (NIV)

Ask

Kids ask questions with such ease and excitement. They have no shame, boundaries or taming limitations when it comes to their curiosity. In fact, there's been a time or two my children have asked inappropriate questions too loudly, producing an abrupt end to our shopping trip! God, being the perfect Father, who never gets tired or embarrassed of our questions, invites us, as His children, into intimate conversations with Him.

Asking God hard and uncomfortable questions does not belittle or offend Him, it shows our trust and humility to share our limitations with a limitless God. In my walk with Christ, I have discovered that my God is big enough for my questions. When you go to someone to ask a question, you are acknowledging that they are a source who has the authority to provide you with an answer. In asking God questions, we acknowledge that Jesus is all powerful, all knowing and all loving.

When my oldest daughter, Syrena, was born nothing went as planned! We were so excited to bring our sweet girl into the world, and because I was measuring big, they thought my due date was wrong. We went to a specialist to affirm the assumption, and after the sonogram, we were asked to go to the counseling office. At that point, we knew something was really wrong. They informed us that she had what's called duodenal atresia, which means she had a blockage in her small intestine. I was huge, but it wasn't because of her due date or the buffet line, it was because of her condition.

Shocked by the report, the doctor continued to share that because of her diagnosis, she would also likely have other abnormalities, like Down syndrome. That was a hard day, as my husband and I were in our early twenties and excited to see our family grow and now we were being hit with the news that struck our vision. Even in the midst of it, we told the professionals that we did not want any further testing because we were trusting God and that no matter what our daughter had to face in life, she would be loved and her purpose would be complete in the Father's hands.

I didn't make it much longer before I found myself in the hospital at thirty-three weeks pregnant. After two days of steroid injections to help build her up, my water broke, and Syrena was born the day she turned thirty-four weeks. She was 4.14 lbs and had no signs of any additional abnormalities! We praised God and soaked up the beauty of her first twenty-four hours, knowing that she would have to undergo surgery the next day, and we would not be able to hold her for a week or more.

Everything went as planned for once, and the surgery was a success! Now we just had to wait another two weeks to bring our sweet baby girl home and get back to what we thought would be a normal life with our preemie. However, after leaving the hospital, it was anything but normal.

By five months old, I had taken Syrena to the pediatrician time and time again. I kept telling them something was wrong with her, and they kept telling me she was fine. She would throw up often after eating and cried all the time. All the time. I was desperate for help and for sleep, but they kept sending me home. As a twenty-four-year-old mom, I didn't know what to do; I just knew something wasn't right. Finally, I demanded they test her, and out of an effort to console this new momma, they obliged.

I watched as they strapped my baby down on a machine that rotated her like a piece of meat to see if the liquid would pass through her intestines. It only took a minute into the test before they said, "There!" They found what's called malrotation. Her intestines were all twisted up inside so she could not process food correctly. She would have died from this condition if they had not caught it in time. She had to have surgery. *Again* . . . our thoughts strayed, "How are we finding ourselves here again, Lord? I don't get it!"

We were doing everything right, by my account. My husband was working for the church, we were there every time the doors were open, we tithed, we prayed, we read our Bibles. "Why?!" We cried and we prayed. Not knowing exactly what to do, we got ourselves around some other believers, and we worshiped. We asked the why questions because God's big

God's big enough for our questions, but sometimes His answer is simply His presence.

enough for our questions, but sometimes His answer is simply His presence.

At that moment, in the middle of tears, fears, worship and questions, God reminded me of my daughter's name: Syrena Mia Gonzales, which means "My Peace in the Battle." All of a sudden, through our prayer time, God gave us this peace that didn't have limits, it didn't offer us answers; instead, it gave us assurance that God was with us.

In the waiting room the day of her surgery, we had no fear or worry, just peace authored by our confidence in our trustworthy God. Finally, the doctor came out and said, "During the surgery we were able to fix the malrotation, but we also discovered a growth on her intestine that we had to remove. The growth was not there in her original surgery, so it must have developed later on. If we had not had this surgery, the growth would not have been detected and could have burst causing all types of internal damage to her vital organs."

All of a sudden our "Why God?" questions turned into a "Wow God!" declaration. He knew all along that He was protecting our daughter, using one thing to get us to see another, and yet He didn't belittle our questions. He didn't chastise our lack of understanding, He just encouraged us to bring *all* of us—our doubts, our fears, our worries, our questions—to all of Him. Is there something that you are afraid to ask God? He's not mad at you. He's not punishing you. He's not waiting for you to mess up. He wants you. All of you.

All of me is what the Lord got in my season of betrayal. History had taught me to ask without fear of reprimand, so I asked God the why questions all over again. "Why did I lose all my friends?" I asked Him one day. He knew I was trying to fix the "problem" (obviously me), so I could have my "friends" back again, but it just wasn't working! The more I tried to be what they wanted me to be, the more I would get hurt.

Jesus responded to my prayers with this prompt in my spirit, "Why do you keep trying to mend what I have broken?" He answered my questions with a question . . . just like a dad, right? I answered Him angrily, "I liked my life!" You'd think at this point in our conversation He'd give me a real answer, but no, another question came in response to my fit: "Would you rather live in the light or in darkness?" Tears began streaming down my face. I didn't respond this time, because I knew He already knew the answer and so did I. So I left well enough alone, took a deep breath and leaned into His loving arms as He comforted my soul. He was and is a friend to the friendless.

Seek

The thing about darkness is that you can't see anything, so you have to rely on memory! My father-in-law went completely blind in his last few years of life. If you moved one thing out of its ordinary spot, like a chair, he would stumble. When the lights are on, it's easy to maneuver the obstacles that are in front of us, but in darkness, nothing can change, even if it's dysfunctional. You need to be in the light to make the changes needed.

After my Father-daughter talk with the Lord, the lights came on and, boy, was everything a mess. I saw things I had allowed, toxic conversations I had entertained, and I also saw that I was not who I was told I was. Although far from perfect, I had been a good friend, loyal, honest, caring and I believed the best in people even when I had been hurt. Stumbling around in the darkness for so long had created a lot of clutter and chaos in my life, but it was familiar to me, so I didn't realize it was dangerous. Just because you are familiar with something doesn't mean it's healthy. So with my eyes wide open, I began to seek order, clarity and help to once again be able to trust.

Seek help. That seems easy, but when you are wounded, the acknowledgment of that wound is the most difficult step in the healing process. After all, if you bring it up, you can no longer ignore it. Also, you don't know who you can trust with your pain. The doubts lingered; however, I pressed through them, and with all the courage I could muster up, I asked someone for help. I immediately regretted it as she began to rehearse all the gossip she had heard about it over the previous few months. That was enough to send me back under the proverbial rock!

Resilient, I inquired to another trusted soul, and in return for my vulnerability, I got no follow-up, no promised phone call or compassionate embrace to nurture me to healing. It hurt and discouragement settled in. Everything in me wanted to throw in the towel, and I had just started. However, one thing I knew, beyond what I felt, is that giving up was not an option for me. Emotions are real, but they don't rule me and my trust was certainly not going to be misplaced in them. After all, what I knew in my heart of hearts is that *Don't misplace your trust in your emotions.* Jesus had already prepared for my healing. He bought and paid for it on the cross over two thousand years ago! Additionally, a good father loves to give answers. So I kept on seeking.

Sometimes your best friends in seasons of pain are the ones who get paid by the hour. I saw a Christian counselor for deeper guidance. It made a difference. I followed through on all the homework he gave me, and I didn't stop there. I showed up to every weekend service at my church, sat on the front row, ready to take notes and I leaned in. I continued in personal devotion, prayer and study of the Word. I showed up to lead my small group, and little by little I'd open up to share deeper places of my own soul. Like physical therapy after a bodily injury, I kept pressing on toward the goal. I kept seeking.

Knock

One day, my kids thought they would be funny and snuck out the back door and ran to the front door to trick me by ringing the doorbell. Here's the thing, though, I know my kids. Like, I really know them. I know their knock, I know their ring. No one lays on the doorbell like that except for my children! The point being, a parent knows their child because of constant proximity, habits and relationship.

Our relationship with the Lord is just like this parent-child connection. There's nothing He wants to withhold from us, and He knows our cry. He won't leave us in trouble, He will answer. We can trust His character and nature. Likewise, as kids, we can know the character of our parents and rest in their arms. Even when a parent doesn't have all the answers, their embrace makes everything OK.

I went to bed praying one particular night. I had a problem, but I knew the Lord had a solution. I was able to cast my cares on Him and sleep even with no answer. When I woke I had this overwhelming sense of gratitude. Sometimes I go to bed with a problem and wake up with a solution. It's like my body and mind are no longer in competition with my spirit, and I can commune with God on a different level. I immediately started to pray and thank God that I could trust Him, and I felt Him say this to me: "You trust me, but I entrust you." The word entrust means to "assign the responsibility for doing something or to put (something) into someone's care or protection."[4]

This, then, is how you ought to regard us: as servants of Christ and as those entrusted with the mysteries God has revealed. Now it is required that those who have been given a trust must prove faithful.
1 Corinthians 4:1-2 (NIV)

The God of the universe entrusts us with secret things when we prove faithful. He gives us responsibility and has confidence that we can hear Him and care and protect the integrity of the task He's given. This totally blows my mind!

Our relationship with God is like a dance: we trust Him, He entrusts us, and this repeats over and over from glory to glory like a beautifully choreographed ballroom routine.

In our pain, we can count on God to give us the next step to healing. We can trust Him with everything, just as we can be entrusted to follow His words to us. This is not to say we will always like what He does or says. I would find myself longing for friendships and would knock on the door, reminding God that I needed people in my circle, but then found myself refusing to let anyone in.

One particular evening, a friend that wasn't super close to me at the time shared some insights with me. I had held her at a distance, afraid that she would get all tangled up in the sticky web of accusations that had been spun around me by the people that had once been close to me. I stood there speechless as she told me things that only God knew were brewing in my heart. I didn't give much emotion, thanked her and jumped in the car to go home. On that ride, I was angry with God and felt that He had betrayed me too by sharing my mess with her. I was supposed to be able to trust God and now even the Lord was sharing my secrets—what a gossip! As I was honest with Him about how I felt about the whole thing, I felt Him say to me, "I know you don't like it, but it's good for you."

Trustworthy friends are a treasure; flaky friends are a train wreck

I had knocked asking for friends, and then I initially rejected the open door. Trustworthy friends are a treasure, but flaky friends are a train wreck, and I hadn't quite recovered from the collision. When we knock, God answers, but we still have to walk through the door. I cautiously entered this friendship, but God blew my tainted expectations out the door! He didn't just give me an amazing friend, He gave me a second family. Slowly, He rebuilt trust in my heart. I found myself able to be open, honest and even have fun and laugh again. I discovered that I was worth more than what I had been receiving and that I was deserving of reciprocal friendships. I learned how to be vulnerable and authentic in all seasons, not just the good ones. I learned that it's OK if not everyone likes you, and when that happens, you are in good company. I learned from Joshua that you may wind up leading the very community that wanted to stone you, so it's better to start learning how to love people beyond their own messed-up opinions and hurtful actions (more about this later). I learned that God is trustworthy, and when all else fails, He will still be there to love us and help us up. I also learned that I want to be trustworthy with other people's pain. When you've been mishandled, choose to handle others well.

Regardless of where you are today, keep asking, seeking and knocking! Keep walking through the doors that the Lord opens up for you. The pathway to God's plan for your life will not disappoint you despite how many twists and turns you may encounter. Stay the course. You can trust and *be trustworthy* because God is trustworthy with all of you!

My Reflections

"Discipline is the bridge between goals and accomplishment."

-Mother Teresa

Let us not become weary in doing good, for at the proper time we will reap a harvest if we do not give up.

Galatians 6:9 (NIV)

Chapter 4
Be Consistent

I appreciate consistency. There's nothing more exhausting than not knowing what person you are going to get from one day to the next. As humans, we crave consistency. If you regularly attend church, where do you sit each week? Same spot, huh? It's just human nature. It's the same with my meal planning. My kids can consistently count on tacos, chicken noodle soup, hamburgers, baked chicken, and spaghetti. Sometimes they love it, and sometimes they say, "That again!"

If truth be told, I have been consistent in my life with both good and bad things. Bad habits are hard to break, and since I have consistently thought poorly of myself for so much of my life, my thoughts have critically damaged my confidence and inhibited my ability to clearly see who I am.

Israel too had this yo-yo of good and bad behavior that produced a dreadful end. If you read through their story, you will see God do a miraculous sign, and then in what seems like five minutes, the people forget, begin to complain, turn their worship to something other than God and compare their inabilities to the perceived strength of their adversaries. Why did ten of the twelve spies spread rumors that infected Israel with fear and disbelief? Comparison. Read it for yourself:

> *But the people who lived there were powerful...*
> *We can't attack those people; they are stronger than we are.*
> *... All the people we saw there are of great size.*
> *... We seemed like grasshoppers in our own eyes, and we*
> *looked the same to them.*
> *Our wives and children will be taken as plunder...*
> *Numbers 13:28, 31–33, 14:3 (NIV)*

All of this negative talk after seeing the Lord defeat Pharaoh with twelve plagues, the classic parting of the Red Sea, water coming out of a rock, a cloud by day and a fire by night leading them, the defeat of the Amalekites and I'm sure I'm missing a few more miraculous moments, but you get the point. What does it take for us to see the consistent goodness of God? He fights for us! What does it take for us to look in the mirror and see victory instead of defeat, beauty instead of ashes, redemption instead of rejection, strength instead of weakness? God will not force us to see what He sees, but our choice to embrace His image or deflect it will determine our suffering or our success. When we are constantly comparing ourselves to

Our choice to embrace God's image or deflect it will determine our suffering or our success.

others, our reflection will never be enough. People were not created for comparison, we were created as companions.

It's easy to look at someone and see what you don't have. Growing up I thought that my older sister was the whole package, and I got left with nothing. She's smart, beautiful, talented, and from my vantage point, my dad's favorite. One day in our twenties we were getting ready to take some pictures and I told her to hurry up because we were going to be late, and she said to me, "That's easy for you to say. You're the pretty one!" I was shocked and thought, "Why didn't anyone tell me that I was the pretty one?"

In the metaphorical line where God would hand out gifts to each person, I always felt He accidentally passed over me leaving me with nothing special. I had no idea that all those years my sister thought of me the way she did, but I had the same thoughts of her. It's interesting to think what might have happened if instead of comparing all those years, we had both focused on complimenting—pulling out the best of each other. If instead of competing for attention, we completed one another by giving each other our basic human needs: to be seen, known and loved.

Oftentimes people want what you have, but they don't want to pay what you've paid for it. In my maturity I can look at another woman that is fit and has a gorgeous physique and think, ya . . . I don't deserve that. When she was at bootcamp at 5 a.m., I was asleep and I loved it! I can celebrate her now, but I know there was a time when I would have hated her for her hard work. When we think like this, it's because we are very aware that we are missing something in our own lives and they have it: that something is consistency.

Think about it. Did this poor woman take something away from us? Is there not enough room at the gym because of her? Is there no celery left in the grocery stores because of her? Did she take this opportunity away from us? No! Our bodies have potential, but it's up to us to pull the potential out of our lives. She didn't take an opportunity away from us. She just didn't settle for what we settled for. She was consistent (if you are "she," I applaud you), but we can choose to be consistent too. Don't worry about the highlight reels of someone else's life; just do the meaningful work of staying the course. Stay steady, persistent, dependable and true! Be Consistent.

Fruitful

Although my season of betrayal in my friendships was rough for me, because I had already maintained a consistent, healthy habit of going to church, reading my Bible daily and praying, I was able to go deeper in my healing through God's direction. As I pressed in, the Word became more alive to me than ever before. I began to get fresh vision and revelation and grew secure in my identity in Christ. I still hang my hat of faith on some of the things that the Lord revealed to me during my healing journey. I had the sweetest, intimate times with the Lord, and He gave me some of the most amazing, loyal friendships that I might not have ever been open to if I hadn't gone through what I went through. In addition, my heart was softer and more compassionate to seeing those hurting around me, resulting in bringing to them the same comfort and healing the Lord had freely given to me. All of this because of my consistency in seeking God.

A spiritually disciplined life leads to fruitful seasons in times of difficulty. God wants us to produce a lifestyle of longevity in our faith by creating spiritual disciplines that will support us in our times of need. It gives me so much pleasure to study how God works. One of the most frustrating things when someone is mad at you or against you is for them to watch you prosper and be joyful. God confuses and spoils the enemy's plans when we are equipped to go to war with His tools! Through Christ, you will have undeniable joy in the midst of pain, you will be stronger because of the assault you endured, you will do things you never thought you could, you will trust again, you will be a better friend and God will use even crooked paths to get you exactly where he wants you to be:

A spiritually disciplined life leads to fruitful seasons in times of difficulty.

> Consider what God has done:
> Who can straighten what he has made crooked?
> Ecclesiastes 7:13 (NIV)

No matter how crooked our path might feel, we are marked by God, secured in His design, made for success and subject to His expressed will. In His faithfulness, God will meet you no matter where you are, so start activating consistent practices that will support your spiritual life now. It's best to have positive routines before a storm-like season interrupts your life.

It's better to exercise before you have a health crisis. At the same time, there's also something to be said about receiving a diagnosis and it spurring you on to healthy living.

Maybe you're in a season right now where it feels like you have so much to work on in your life that it's just overwhelming! I want to encourage you to not go into bondage by trying to work on thirty things at one time. You'll just feel defeated and give up. Ask God to highlight those top toxic areas of your life so you can focus on replacing bad habits with new beneficial habits that will bring you health. A helpful tip is to share the areas that God is highlighting to you with people whom you trust. They can be on guard to help protect you from falling into the trap of complacency.

Pruning

Joshua and Caleb knew all too much about pain, threats, toxic relationships and the confusion that comes from fear. As we learned in the previous chapter, their whole community was talking about stoning them just because they gave a good report about the explorations of the land they wanted to inhabit. Good does not mean easy. It was most definitely going to be challenging to walk out their conquest, but Joshua and Caleb believed in the power and promises of God. They knew they could partner with Him and win! They were committed to consistently growing.

Good does not mean easy.

I can't imagine the pain of having to walk around and live with a community that I knew hated me to the point that they wanted me dead. However, I do know all too well how it feels to be in a community where you just don't feel valued. It may seem small, but at the time, it was big to me. In the midst of the awkward transition of my onboarding, during the relationally crushing season I shared with you, one of my team members said something to me that cut me: "You are not a leader. At best, you are a manager of things."

These words were so damaging to my already fragile and fatigued emotions. I felt naked in a room full of people. I don't know what her intentions were, but it didn't even matter because I had ingested so much toxic talk from people whom I thought were friends that those words were immediately deadly venom to me. Everything affirmed the notion that I nurtured: no one liked me. To show up for work each day was a battle. I needed to be pruned.

I am the true vine, and My Father is the vinedresser. Every branch in Me that does not bear fruit He takes away; and every branch that bears fruit He prunes, that it may bear more fruit.
John 15:1-2 (NKJV)

To prune means to cut off dead or unwanted parts.[5] My father-in-law had diabetes and once suffered from a gangrene infection in his toe. He was being treated in the hospital, but the fact was that if they did not remove some of his toes, the infection was going to spread throughout his entire body. The gangrene killed the cells in his toes, but it had the potential to take his life.

Now my father-in-law had a choice to make: he could keep his toes or keep his life. He chose life, but in that he still had to heal, he sacrificed a part of himself that had brought him stability and he had to relearn how to walk. I know it wasn't easy for him, but I'm glad he did it. It added years to his life that were so impactful for us all. He saw many more people give their lives to the Lord, he got to see my husband and I get married . . . so much life happened because he was willing to cut off what was killing him.

This is why God prunes us. Our sinful nature wants to cause us death, but God, if we allow Him, will cut off what's killing us. However, sometimes in life we say to God, "No! I've always had these toes. I'm not cutting them off. They've been good to me. They were with me when I took my first steps and when I learned how to dance. I have never gone anywhere without them." And even though they are black, infected and smelly, all we can think of is that they are mine. "I've always had them, and I'm not changing."

I had some of the same thoughts when the Lord pruned my friendships. Even though they were killing my confidence and damaging my trust, I didn't want to have them pruned out of my life. Finally, after I reluctantly released the damaged branches from the trunk of my tree, I began to heal. Just as my father-in-law had to let go of his toes and relearn how to walk, I had to let go of friendships and relearn how to trust. I had to be committed to consistent growth even to the point of releasing what was comfortable to me.

Isolation wanted to take me over, but God had other plans. As the Lord gave my secrets to ones that He knew I could trust, He began to show me that He would bring beauty from my pain. God gave me a true friend that was not only good company but also someone who defended me, loved me, never gave an ear to gossip and not once asked me what happened. She didn't care about knowing the gossip but just genuinely cared about knowing me.

A friend loves at all times, and a brother is born for adversity.
Proverbs 17:17 (ESV)

Through a year of breakups, I also experienced breakthroughs. Hurts had been oozing out of my life affecting every relationship, my leadership and my emotional health, but now the healing power of Jesus strengthened what remained. I relearned how to think, walk, talk, care, love, lead, let people in, set boundaries, be open, and discover the beauty of true friendship and sisterhood. When we are broken, pain seeps out of us, but when healed, we bear fruit. Like a tree planted by water, even in a time of drought, we will have green leaves, able to yield fruit and prosper in whatever we do (Psalm 1:3). It is only through our consistency in seeking after truth and light that we can be healed.

When we are broken, pain seeps out of us, but when healed, we bear fruit.

Grow

What are you holding on to that is causing an infection throughout your body, soul and spirit? Is it a stone that someone hurled at you? How about wounding words spoken to you? Maybe it's the comparison that keeps you in a constant place of defeat or sin that you just can't seem to break away from. Is it a victim mentality that justifies where you are today because of the injustice that happened in your yesterday? Is it manipulation that you embraced as a survival tactic in your youth, but now it's hurting every relationship you have? You can hold on to it, nurture it, make excuses for it, support it, but it will not support you. It will take you over, and it will kill you. It will kill your future. It will kill your relationships, and it will kill your potential.

Pruning is a natural process, and when we consistently embrace it, God will grow us! Some good friends of mine own a tree trimming business. They often have to cut down trees because they are dead or trim them if they are healthy. They once shared that at times, a tree looks good on the outside, but on the inside, it is rotten. They will talk to the owners about what is happening on the inside of the tree, but the owners will often argue with them saying, "This tree has fruit; it looks healthy." Unfortunately for many, regret comes after a storm as they see their tree they once protected come down on their homes they left unprotected. Once uprooted, they can see that it's black with rot on the inside. The truth is that we can outwardly appear good and even have some limited fruit, but we can be dying on the inside!

I think for us, as Christians, sometimes it's hard to challenge our issues because we know when something is sin, like harboring offense, so we doctor it up with a bunch of Christian words so we can give ourselves permission to not deal with it. I see a great deal of this in the church world. Offenses are caused by a myriad of things like something said or perceived harshly, being accused of doing something wrong, and being overlooked for a position or opportunity. When this happens, instead of being honest and going to the person, we become critical of their leadership, outwardly expressing gratitude but inwardly harboring resentment. The sad part is that we are only deceiving ourselves and giving the infection permission to spread throughout our entire body. Just because you know it's a sin does not mean that you are separated from it.

When we avoid dealing with offense, we give the infection of hurt permission to spread through our entire body because we did not want to confront our feelings. By not dealing with the active sin, we only deceive ourselves. The scriptures tell us that even the demons knew that Jesus was Lord. This should give us great caution as it relates to what we think we know. Just because we can repeat scripture, does not exempt us from struggling with sin. Truth be told, undealt with disappointment leads to bitterness. If a religious spirit is at play, it will disable us from admitting the truth. Instead of being honest, we cover up our pain to protect dysfunction instead of revealing it. Hear this: it's OK to admit that you are hurt. As much as you want to be

Undealt with disappointment leads to bitterness.

OK, you are not. Ignoring your infection will not make it go away, it will make it spread.

We must consistently reassess what we are holding on to and recognize sin so we can let go of it.

Good discipline

You can't conceal to heal. What's inside of you will seep out of you so make the choice to let it out in a way that brings healing. We have to stop talking *You can't conceal to heal.* Christian and start being Christian! That means consistently having hard conversations, letting go of offenses, victimization and the should have, could have, would haves of life. We all have them. It's time to confess. You were hurt, you've let things take root, you made a bad decision, but now you are going to reveal it and surrender it to God. The Lord will redeem it when we bring it to Him. Even the time you've wasted on it can be redeemed for His glory! When we bring all of this into the light, the enemy has nothing to torture us with!

My child, don't reject the LORD's discipline,
and don't be upset when he corrects you.
For the LORD corrects those he loves,
just as a father corrects a child in whom he delights.
Proverb 3:11-12 (NLT)

God gave me this scripture when I started in full-time ministry, and I have held it so close to me. Due to the many rejections I experienced growing up, I could easily interpret good criticism meant to make me better as a rejection of who I am. Pruning seasons are good seasons, but they don't always feel good. They are the seasons that are responsible for the abundance of fruit in your future days. This scripture gave me a different outlook on correction, delivering comfort and even hope in times when I would receive it. It is because the Lord loves us that He will send discipline to us. If He didn't see potential in us, He wouldn't bother, but He does, and He wants us to grow. Our heavenly Father does the hard things that every good parent does: He disciplines!

Even though we don't want others to see our failures, they will. Even though we don't want to acknowledge our sin, it won't just go away on its own. So when the pruners come (and they will), we need to remember it's not the pruner's job to decide if the branch feels like it's being cut or it's being pruned. I felt cut when I was told I wasn't a leader. It *It's not the pruner's job to decide if the branch feels like it's being cut or it's being pruned.* produced a deep wound, and for a while, it caused an infection of insecurity to run through my veins, but that was my choice. It was also my choice to make changes.

As leaders, it's important that we are always pruning others from a pure heart and motive, but as the ones receiving corrections, we get to decide if we want to shrivel up and die or if we want to be on the other side of the branch: the side that grows, learns and gives fruit. We often have to choose to "Chew up the meat and spit out the bones." The fact is we are all a hot mess, and we are going to go through some stuff, but with some wisdom and the gift of the Holy Spirit, we can bear good fruit. Additionally, when people are harsh with you, remember that the Lord is so gentle, as noted in 1 Peter 5:7. "Live carefree before God; he is most careful with you" (MSG).

Years later, I took this team member aside as she was getting ready to exit the team and I asked her an honest question: "Do you remember telling me that I'm not a good leader? I just wanted to ask you if you've seen any improvement in my leadership over the last few years." I don't know how many times I had replayed her prior words in my head, and to be real with you, I wasn't sure if I was going to like her response, but I felt in my heart to ask, to get clarity and closure. To my surprise she said, "Is that all you've heard me say to you? I've said so many wonderful things about you and to you since that one moment." This was not at all what I was expecting! I really hadn't heard her say those wonderful things she said. It's amazing how our minds are trained to only hear negative things. I can receive one hundred compliments and only recall the one critical thing someone said.

Remember the old saying, "Sticks and stones may break my bones, but words will never harm me"? Well, it's a total lie! Words do harm us. They cut us, and they will steal peace from us if we do not know who we are. In your life, you will receive criticism, some productive and some that you shouldn't take to bed with you! The key to success in receiving criticism is knowing who you are. And knowing who you are comes from consistently seeking God and reflecting His image through the pruning process. We all have things to work on, but knowing who you are brings security to your confidence in times of refinement.

Knowing who you are brings security to your confidence in times of refinement.

I wonder if Joshua and Caleb had any sleepless nights after the rumors and harsh criticisms they received? I wonder what it felt like getting up each morning, continuing with their job routines and staying in a community with people who wanted to get rid of them. We don't know all the details of their stories, but what we do know is that they were faithful and they were consistent. They worked through their pain. They showed up.

Honesty time. It's just you and I, so with integrity of heart I ask, who or what cut you? Was it your community, spouse, parents, coworker, significant other, teacher, sibling, cousin, coach, aunt, uncle, grandparents, pastor or a leader? Will you allow those deadly thoughts, lingering words or harsh betrayals to slice you up, or will you release them, allowing the damaged limbs to fall void to the ground so you can bear more fruit? Will you protect the dysfunction in your life, or will you humbly allow others to come along and prune places in your life that are capable of causing death?

The choice is yours, friend, so choose wisely. For me, I did what I always do: I grew! I stayed consistent. I asked God to search my heart and give me the path for change. I chewed up the meat and spit out the bones. I confessed my hurts, and in doing so, God removed my shame. I showed up, even when I didn't feel like it. I stayed when I wanted to run. I worked diligently on the internal things that needed to be trimmed. I did the hard things, and I continue to do them. Let's be honest, if we want to bear fruit, we will always need to be pruned. No matter what's being hurled your way, keep doing you in a way that will produce the best version of you. Be consistent with the things that grow you. Never give up, for God surely won't!

Consistently look to God to know your worth. Consistently allow your life to be pruned so you can be fruitful. Consistently embrace how God wired you and made you. Consistently encourage others to greatness. Consistently dive into the Word of God so it can shape you. Consistently pray to be conformed into the image of Christ. Consistently confess your sins so you may be healed. *Be consistent.*

My Reflections

"Insecure leaders think everything is about them, and as a result, every action, every piece of information, every decision is put through their filter of self-centeredness."

-John C. Maxwell

Love your neighbor as yourself. There is no commandment greater than these.

Mark 12:31 (NIV)

Chapter 5
Be Confident

I've heard people say that they are good at loving others, but they are not good at loving themselves. The truth is that we can't love other people well until we love ourselves. No matter how hard we try, our goodness to others will be tainted by our own unconscious internal needs. God wants us to love as He loves and that includes loving ourselves. When we do so, we can love people the way that He does, which is why we have been given the command in Mark 12:31. Right now you may not love yourself enough, so if you were to love others as you love yourself, you may be treating people pretty awfully. It's out of security and godly confidence that we can truly focus our attention on others, honoring them with pure motives as Jesus did.

I'm passionate about confidence because I have been the most insecure person on the planet, and I've seen the effects that it can have on your calling, life, family, relationships, career and ministry. Confidence is something that we must walk into, or it will cause us to hide, run over people, kill our joy, steal relationships and hinder our growth.

Most of my life I have walked into every room like everybody hates me. I was always working from a deficit because I hated myself before I ever walked in. I projected my own thoughts about myself, my insecurities, onto innocent bystanders.

Being an introvert, I've had way too much time in my head to say bad things to myself or to take hurtful things others have said to me and nurture those words until I believed them or became them. I've made up lots of stories in my mind as well. If you didn't say "Hi" in the hallway, I would have thought through every conversation we've ever had, trying to see if I might have offended you. If you didn't invite me to lunch with the other girls, I would wonder if someone was talking negatively about me. If you ask to meet with me, I prepared myself for the hundreds of things that I may have done wrong. It was simply self-absorbed thinking and *exhausting*.

What would happen if we all walked into every room with confidence? The world wants to make us a victim of approval addiction by thinking that everyone is against us, that we have to earn acceptance, but we are set apart from the world! Paul says it best:

Here is a trustworthy saying that deserves full acceptance: Christ Jesus came into the world to save sinners—of whom I am the worst. I Timothy 1:15 (NIV)

Even in our worst state, God thought we were worth saving! We are fully accepted by Him, in that we can be confident. So we need to learn to do the same. Let's love ourselves well so we can love others well. Honoring our creator by reciprocating His actions toward us.

Insecurity versus Confidence

Insecurity demands us to give attention to our own needs, whereas confidence allows us to live free of these self-focused, restrictive thoughts and behaviors so we can give better care to the people around us. I think we all have seasons or areas of life where insecurity creeps in, but we can't live life there. Insecurity is a thief of our time and God's purpose for our lives.

> *Insecurity demands us to give attention to our own needs.*

Insecurity begs to be noticed, demands credit and soaks up praise. It makes everyone around us work so much harder to compensate for our lack. It always has to be right, because being wrong would expose vulnerability, so it blames your failures on other people and never allows you to take responsibility for your life. It makes you defensive instead of open to positive criticism. Insecurity questions every decision you make and other people's motives, leaving you up at night worrying about people's perceptions and the uncertainty of your future.

Insecurity can also take the opposite effect. It can make you hide, people please, and work tirelessly to be what everyone else wants you to be. You're the first one to volunteer, the last one to leave, but you also feel like nothing was good enough at the end of the day. This can lead to resentment and toxic behaviors.

On the other hand, godly confidence serves people and serves you. When you're confident, you don't have to fight if your name is on trial—your character defends itself.

Confidence has peace in every storm, loves seeing other people win, apologizes quickly and seeks to mend hearts, it does not protect appearances. Confidence doesn't boast because it already knows its worth. It serves out of a heart for God that fosters a deep seeded joy. Confidence is built through our own beliefs in who Christ is and how He sees you.

We all want confidence, but it is often misunderstood. The Hebrew word for "confidence" radically means "to be open."

To truly be confident, we must confide in a confidant to expose what the enemy wants to conceal.

This shows us that the biblical context and understanding of confidence is where nothing is hidden, one feels safe.[6] Confidence equals a posture of trust and transparency. Similarly, a confidant is one who can be trusted.[7] To truly be confident, we must confide in a confidant to expose what the enemy wants to conceal. Isn't it just like God to wrap such a vital part of our identity around our ability to communicate to others what's inside of us? Community was always a part of God's plan for us from the beginning of time. He is coming back for a community, the church, and He desires for us to grow in love for one another. You can't love someone you don't know, and you can't be truly loved by people that don't know you.

Loving Yourself

To be loved by others, we need to be known by them, but it can be hard to fully share yourself with other people, especially if you don't like what you see in the mirror. So start by loving yourself. When we are critical of our personalities and looks, we are missing a deeper understanding of our design. Here's a truth to grab ahold of: God, the creator of the universe, uniquely handcrafted us for His glory. That means when we bash ourselves, we are insulting God's design. God doesn't want you to be someone else! He wants you to look to Him to clearly see who He has designed you to be. That's why the sin of comparison is running so rampant today. Our view of ourselves can be so dysfunctional, as we aren't looking to God to know who we are; instead, we are making a god of other people by giving them unhealthy attention that breeds comparison and envy. Do you realize that it was envy that crucified Christ? (Matthew 27:18)

As women, it's important for us to have the right view of ourselves so we can operate out of security and cheer each other on to greatness. I don't know about you, but I do not want to grieve the heart of God, and I can imagine how insulting it is for the Creator to watch His creation stand in front of a mirror and hate what they see. Meanwhile, instead of growing our character and discovering our purpose, we are the biggest bully we've ever faced. Telling yourself that you are not beautiful, pulling your hair out, cutting because it's the only way to control your pain, talking down to yourself or belittling your potential are just a few examples of how far we go to quench our own confidence.

When my youngest was in first grade, I began to see a difference in her behavior and attitude toward herself. You need to understand that Kya is so confident. She's always been very independent and I just love that about her, so her countenance concerned me. One day I told her she was beautiful, and she told me she wasn't. It shocked me! She said, "You're just saying that because you are my mom!" Then I would tell her she was smart, and she would list all the reasons why she wasn't. I asked questions, but I couldn't get to the root of the issue. I walked the hallway of our home many nights praying and interceding for her, asking God for wisdom.

Finally, right after school ended for summer break, we were standing in the kitchen and she told me she was ugly. A righteous anger came over me, and I picked her up, sat her on the counter, pinned her down and eye to eye sternly questioned her, "Who told you that?" Tears immediately began to flow as she shared how a girl in her class had bullied her and told her that she was ugly! This momma wanted to go beat someone up, but instead, I used my energy to begin to rebuild what had been broken.

I'm here to ask you today: Who told you that? You are not who you think you are or who you were told you are! The very first woman, Eve, struggled with the battle of voices too. In Genesis 3 it shares how the devil intrigued her and tricked her with questions and good desires that were perverted by his intent to make her sin. After she fell for his schemes, she ate of the fruit that was forbidden and her eyes were open. Until this moment of her life, she lived naked and completely unashamed; now, she hid from the one that gave her life. However, no matter how much we want to hide from God, He sees us! God questioned Eve, "Who told you that you were naked?" But He didn't stop there. He clothed her, He covered her and He protected her. He transformed her thinking about herself by securing her identity as His beloved daughter, who would be loved no matter what mistakes she would make.

Insecurity can drive us to try to cover up in hopes we will measure up.

Maybe you can relate to Eve's feelings of being naked and ashamed. Insecurity can drive us to try to cover up in hopes we will measure up, but confidence is lived out in the open. In our naked truth we are still covered by the love, grace, forgiveness and protection of God.

Therefore do not throw away your confidence, which has a great reward.
Hebrews 10:35 (ESV)

If we want confidence, we have to stop giving it away so easily. I'm going to tell you the things I told my baby girl as we began to rebuild her confidence. Every word that is spoken to you does not have to be accepted by you. Hurting people hurt people. When life hands out a cruel moment, hand it over to God. He approves of you! Measure everything against the Word of God before you assign it worth, and when you make a mistake, remember that God loves you no matter what. My friend, do not be shaken—you might be one mistake away from an idea that can change everything. Stay open, stop questioning every decision you've made and don't allow the words of others to define your success. God sees potential in you!

Every word that is spoken to you does not have to be accepted by you.

Measure everything against the Word of God before you assign it worth.

Overcompensating

Once I had intense pain in my right shoulder that would come and go. I kept thinking that it would just eventually go away, but it didn't. In fact, it got worse. I continued on with life as normal, minus working out because I just thought it would make it worse. I would catch myself doing things with my left arm, which was so awkward because I'm right-handed, but I was trying to avoid any additional pain. At one point, I thought maybe my shoulder was out of place and that I just needed to have it reset to get it back to normal. I finally made my way to the doctor months after the pain had begun.

After X-rays the doctor told me I had what's called bursitis, which is inflammation of the bursa tissues, because I had done an activity that my body did not have the strength to support. To make matters worse, the doctor asked me, "How did you get this injury? I've seen professional baseball players with this before. What do you do?" as he looked at my 5'3-on-a-good day-stature. Ugh . . . the dreaded question. What do you do? I had a realization: I got the injury baptizing people. I was so embarrassed. I wanted to lie so badly, but I didn't want to spend the extra time repenting before I went to bed so I just went with the truth. "I'm a pastor. I'm pretty sure that this happened when I was baptizing people on Easter Sunday." The doctor said, "Well, that's a first for me." Great! Just the words of comfort I was looking for. To make matters worse, fixing the problem wasn't going to be easy. It would require a pain regiment and physical therapy. It would require me putting weight on the very area that was causing me so much pain, the very thing I had been avoiding for months!

Have you ever taken on a spiritual task that you weren't prepared for or walked into a battle without any preparation? Have you been caught overcompensating in an area of life trying to make up or cover up a place of pain, masking your insecurities with all the wrong activities? My avoidance of the root of the pain had caused me to delay the healing process. In addition, it caused me to lose mobility in that area of my body. It caused me to overcompensate in other areas as a result of my needless delays.

I believe we do the same with pain from insecurity. We avoid it and overcompensate so we can ignore or cover up what's really going on! You can recognize this type of behavior in your life by asking yourself these questions:

- ♥ Do I have a constant need to prove myself?
- ♥ Do I have to be the loudest voice in the room?
- ♥ Do I use humor to distance and deflect?
- ♥ Do I find myself name-dropping, having to one-up people in conversation or constantly sharing my accomplishments in hopes of elevating my status?
- ♥ Do I have to get praise and credit to feel validated in my worth?
- ♥ Do I project authority and operate in high drive, yet long for approval?
- ♥ Do I have a problem backing down, even when I know I'm wrong?
- ♥ Do I work my way into relationships with people through flattery or buying them gifts?

If you said yes to any of these, you likely are overcompensating for an undealt with injury. You are avoiding and delaying your healing and have likely lost the proper function of your godly character. This is not to say that using your gifts like leadership, generosity or humor is wrong, but honestly ask yourself if you are using them for the right reasons. Love corresponds with issues of the heart (we'll learn more about this in chapter 8). Do a heart check by asking why you are doing these things. Are you doing them to be:

- ♥ Invited to something
- ♥ Accepted by a group or a person
- ♥ Thoughtful
- ♥ Obedient to the Lord's prompting

Your truthful answer will give you a greater understanding of where you are and how to move forward. Next, I'm going to say two words, and I want you to ask yourself how the words make you feel. Do they scare you, do you long for them, do they make you cringe, do you want one without the other or do they bring up feelings of hurt or humiliation?

- ♥ Vulnerability: the capability of being physically or emotionally wounded.[8]
- ♥ Authenticity: being true to one's own personality, spirit or character.[9]

Possibly, one word has steered you away from the other. Maybe, like the unhealed version of me, you hunger for authentic relationships, but the thought of being vulnerable, or vulnerable again, makes you shrink back into a counterfeit confidence that overcompensates in hopes to hide who and where you actually are.

Unfortunately, there's no magic pill I can offer you to undo the pain, untangle the mess or flip the switch from insecure to confident. It will only happen when you take the risk of vulnerability to produce the desired outcome of authenticity. When we are real with our pain by facing it, we can apply Jesus to every affected area of our lives, and it will bring the added weight that we need for healing. While painful at times, the right weight brings positive pressure to build strength, leaving us more powerful than before we were injured.

It's possible that the mirror reflects images you'd rather not see right now, but what if you could see something totally different? Do you know that mirrors reflect the opposite of an image as light hits the subject? Here's some food for thought: as the light of Christ hits your situation, it may just have some adverse consequences on what you see in yourself. For example, at first glance, you may see a gossip, but brought into the light, your communication gift can be used for transformative conversations that build instead of break. If you notice hints of depression, discouragement or criticism, clarity in sight can bring forth an encouraging, conquering, hopeful spirit in you. Do you catch a glimpse of a manipulator that ultimately ruins every relationship and leaves you feeling dirty? Illuminated, you can transform into a real friend that's not in it for what she can get from it, but loves as she is loved. Light transforms our reflections.

You cannot speak to what you choose to ignore, but what you choose to ignore will speak through you.

Healing

Healing from your insecurity is a choice, and it starts with your acknowledgment of the emotional and often spiritual pain that you are in. You cannot speak to what you choose to ignore, but what you choose to ignore will speak through you. It will be seen by others in the way you treat them, use them, appease them, run over them or how you're a doormat to them. No matter your end of the spectrum, your insecurity will seep out of you.

God has given us a tool to confront insecurity once we have acknowledged it: the belt of truth. The reason that this piece of armor, the belt, was chosen to describe truth was because it is thought that our emotions are housed in our stomachs. Have you ever been sick to your stomach over a situation? The gut is made up of our stomach, esophagus, intestines and mouth, and it is often referred to as our "second brain."[10] This second brain truly takes on thinking of its own. It is an epicenter for trauma, housing every emotion without restraint. The second brain manifests pain from emotion, and because of its connection to the mouth, it speaks from feelings that are not necessarily true. This second brain literally has a mind of its own! God prescribes us to apply the pressure of truth to every emotion we feel, tightening the belt to produce health. We must realize that truth is vital to health and that emotions are real, but they don't have to have a mind of their own.

Emotions are real, but they don't have to have a mind of their own.

Sincere hearts can authentically share the veracity of our emotions no matter how sad, ugly, or painful they may be, so we can apply God's Word to those tender places. By doing this, we give all of ourselves to God, no longer having to self-protect by telling ourselves lies to make us feel better about it all.

Affecting Others

When we lack confidence, we often end up blaming and hurting others, even God. When operating in insecurity, I want to challenge the character of God instead of developing the character within. I've asked why questions and played the "if only" game to no avail. I naturally project blame and place accusations onto others rather than acknowledging the liability I've become. I don't want to be corrected or confronted. I don't like change. I wish to go up to bat, but I don't want to accept the required coaching on the sidelines. Even in all of this, God is big enough for our questions, honesty, accusations, disappointments, hang-ups and habits, but we have to be big enough, humble enough for His answers and determined enough to change.

Through honest conversations with the Lord, I've realized that in my hurt, I've hurt people. My insecurities, at times, caused me to overcompensate, resulting in unintentionally hurting innocent bystanders in my attempts to achieve, be accepted and appease those whom I wanted to be approved by. We have all stained the journal of someone else's life with the tears we have caused. I have realized how I haven't shown up for someone or how I didn't see them in their pain because I was so overwhelmed by my own. It makes me sad, but it also makes me want to be better!

When we operate from a confident standpoint, we are able to rise from disappointment in ourselves and others, as Joshua teaches us. Assumingly frustrated, delayed by the choices and disobedience of others and finding himself just going through the motions of life, the Lord suddenly shifts Joshua's position.

In an unexpected event, caused by Moses's negative actions, the Lord promotes Joshua as the leader of Israel (Numbers 20). I can imagine that this was both difficult and exciting for Joshua. He deeply loved Moses and respected him. He was often referred to as Moses's assistant to imply that they not only worked together but that Joshua would often be by his side, ready and willing to do whatever was needed. By this time, he had proven himself faithful, he had become a man tested, tried, approved and now appointed.

As much of a disappointment it had to be to Moses to not go into the Promised Land, it also had to be a joy for him to see someone that had served him so well take the lead. In Deuteronomy 3:28, the Lord commanded Moses to do two things that we should all take note of: encourage and strengthen Joshua. When people go through hardships and seasons of change, as believers, we are commissioned by God to build their confidence by giving them encouragement and strength.

Buddy Tape

On another normal day, I went out to my patio and there was a strange man standing there. I stood in shock as he moved forward to attack me. Before I knew it, my body went into autopilot and I positioned myself in a Karate Kid stance by throwing up my eagle arms and planting one foot on the ground and the other in the air ready to take the enemy down. I know what you are thinking, and the answer is no. No, I have not ever taken any karate lessons, but my son took karate for a year when he was five, and I faithfully went to every session. Some things are caught and not taught.

Back to the patio, with all my force, I kicked this audacious trespasser with my foot and nailed that sucker right between the eyes. I knocked him plum out. The cops came right away and arrested him for bodily injury and trespassing. My toe was shattered from the incident, but my life was saved!

Well, that sounds so much more entertaining than the truth that I was cleaning the patio in a hurry before company came over, and I stubbed my toe on a chair so hard that it completely broke.

I had never broken a bone before, and I never want to again! Who knew that such a small part of your body could cause you so much pain. To top it off, when you have a broken toe, there's not much you can do. The first step is to tie your broken toe to a healthy stable toe, and over time, the bone fuses back together. This method is called "buddy taping." Now, I've had friends that did not apply this method to their broken toe, and it resulted in their toe healing crooked. Listen, I don't mean to be vain, but I think that I have pretty toes. There's no way I'd take any chances of not getting this toe back in alignment, so I kept them tied together for the next eight weeks.

The same is true when we are building spiritual confidence: we can read the Word of God and we can try to do the right things, but unless we have a buddy, someone that we can be accountable to, we can end up not having the right support that we need to walk securely. We can end up not healing properly or growing in the wrong direction or getting hurt all over again! You don't want funny-looking toes or faulty faith!

I can imagine that Joshua experienced a great deal of brokenness during his forty years of slavery. He was freed, but how would he know how to truly live free? He drew strength, wisdom and understanding from his mentor, Moses, and his comrade, Caleb. Moses built in him such a powerful confidence simply by pulling potential out of his life. He knew Joshua was capable of handling hard labor, so he entrusted him with warrior-like activities. The things my pastor would entrust me with would always shock me over the years. The fact that she would trust me with such important projects built my confidence. I never thought I was capable of doing the things she would ask me to do, but I trusted her and would rise to the potential she saw in me. Likewise, Caleb's boldness in adversity gave Joshua the security and poise to stand for his convictions even if that meant it would be the two of them standing alone.

Similarly, the only thing that gave relief to the pain of my brokenness was when it was buddy taped to the stable toe next to it because it took the pressure off of my injury. There was a support and strength that was drawn from the toe that was functioning properly. Apart from Christ, we are all broken and separated from God's design for our lives. When we come into relationship with God, He gives us the gift of a Christian community so we can grow in confidence. That's what happens when we tie ourselves to the godly friendships that are centered on the Word of God and invite the Holy Spirit to guide and direct us. Allowing other believers to speak into our lives gives us the right support and strength to grow and heal in the right direction. I'm not saying it's easy. I know all too well how hard it is to trust someone in times of pain, but it will surprisingly give you relief. You will be able to process, breathe and laugh again.

After eight weeks of being taped up, I could wear my heels again! As a pastor, I often encounter people that are not willing to commit to the process of healing. They settle for a fake confidence that puts on a show at church for an hour and fifteen minutes and then immediately fall back into bad habits and bad thinking the moment they leave the church doors. Once at a small group, a friend admitted, "I feel like a fake!" That was a day she truly taped herself to our sisterhood. She acknowledged her pain, anger, resentment, and regret that she had been carrying on her own for too many years to count. She kept showing up, dressed up, but that night she didn't try to mask anything. It was a night of freedom and healing.

Being buddy taped requires you to go a different way than where you want to go. It demands trust and security, knowing that even though it may not feel good, it's good for you. A good friend will call you out and a better friend will receive it and make it right.

> *A good friend will call you out and a better friend will receive it and make it right.*

Our human nature wants to take shortcuts to confidence by building it in isolation, but it only leaves us more lost than ever. When we face things alone, it will take five years to get over something that happened in five minutes. The longer we delay by doing things our own way, by ourselves, for ourselves, the longer the enemy has to torment us with it. If a broken bone heals crooked, the only way to fix it is to re-break the bone. I don't know about you, but having experienced what a broken bone feels like, I just want to get it right the first time no matter the discomfort or effort it might cause.

Public Pain

Which brings me to the second step in healing a broken toe, the all but lovely podiatry shoe. Mine happened to be royal blue and white. Really? Why don't they make them all black so they can somewhat match something? I had to wear this lovely accessory for our Father's Day celebration, to church, to my small group, in the office and *everywhere* else I went. It was a big, obnoxious reminder of my run-in with the chair. This shoe told everyone of my shortcomings and begged for tons of questions. One of the hardest things, when you are going through a season of pain, is to have to walk through it publicly. Even the most secure person can feel their confidence being shaken in these vulnerable moments.

Feeling exposed by breakups, divorce, loss, bankruptcy, a wayward child, social disaster or death can challenge our ability to go through normal day-to-day activities without hurtful moments, comments and debilitating thoughts. It can be hard to have the will to get out of bed and go on with life. Times like these require us to become desperate enough to care less about our reputation and more about our healing. True confidence is not externally driven, it's internally built.

There are always going to be the haters with opinions, harmful words or even well-meaning people who just don't know what to say. They aren't going anywhere, but we are, so let's get to higher thinking so we can live out a higher calling.

Get to higher thinking so you can live a higher calling!

One thing I love about Joshua is that he didn't try to change Israel, he left that to God. In fact, he not only continued to walk confidently, he loved confidently. He didn't leave after betrayal, he became more loyal. His confidence was not defined by external affairs, it was built and rewarded by his unwavering beliefs and relationship with the Lord.

True confidence is not externally driven, it's internally built.

The accusations of men screamed loudly the day Joshua and Caleb brought the good report, but what saddens me even more is that the accusations were coming from the church. We have enough antagonists on the outside of the church that we need to fiercely protect and love each other well on the inside. Friend, as the church we are known as the bride of Christ, so let's walk like a confident bride: beautiful, spotless, and with grace. Let's not throw criticism around, gossip or spread fear like wildfire. Let's be known as a sisterhood that defends, honors and protects!

Seek Your Approval from God!

For am I seeking the approval of man, or of God?
Or am I trying to please man? If I were still trying
to please man, I would not be a servant to Christ.
Galatians 1:10 (ESV)

You will never please everyone, *so stop trying!* This is not to
say we treat people badly, but rather that even if they treat us
badly, we are confident to love as Jesus loves and walk
securely. Seek God's approval, and you will receive it. His
approval is the only approval that can sustain us. Even in our
worst state, Jesus still gave His life for us. He didn't wait until
after I got my act together to love me and give His life for me.
No, He did it knowing every horrible thing I would ever do or
think! If that is not love and acceptance, I don't know what is.

We have to understand that it's not through our own might
that we can do anything. It's not by my might, nor by my
power, but by the spirit of God that we can accomplish all
things! (Zechariah 4:6) I love this scripture: "The Lord will
fulfill his purpose for me; your steadfast love, O Lord, endures
forever." Psalm 138:8 (ESV).

It takes all the pressure off of you when we believe that He will
fulfill His purpose in us. If God is in control, we can be
confident in the outcome.

Joshua was able to stay and stand in his community because he
got this: we have the acceptance and love of Christ. He had
unshakable confidence in the Lord and that empowered him
to not cave to the pressure. We combat the fear of rejection by

understanding and receiving the acceptance of Jesus and the fullness of His unconditional love for us.

You can't change the haters, but you don't have to let their voices change you.

If you've been feeling overwhelmed, I want to encourage you to stay above reproach, above the lies and above the shadows of insecurity. You can't change the haters, but you don't have to let their voices change you. Let God be God and do what He does. He will fight for you! Be at peace. In quiet confidence, you will find rest.

The LORD will fight for you, and you have only to be silent.
Exodus 14:14 (ESV)

Joshua, now close to eighty years old, had to remember who he was forty years ago. He stepped into leadership once again, regaining confidence and the Lord encouraged him every step of the way:

Do not be afraid; do not be discouraged, for the Lord your God will be with you wherever you go. Joshua 1:9 (NIV)

Jesus knows what it's like to be humiliated and to walk through pain publicly. He was stripped naked and exposed to everyone, beaten and bruised. He was mocked, labeled and ridiculed. They even stole His clothes and gambled for them (Matthew 27:35). Many of the people who had welcomed Him and listened to His teachings were now a part of His betrayal. If anyone could have church hurt, it was Jesus, but He didn't leave the church. He became the chief cornerstone for it. While on the cross, He remembered the songs of old from Psalm 22:2. He forgave, even when He felt forsaken. He even stood up for those that rejected Him. Jesus gave us an example of unstoppable confidence, and just as He rose on the third day, God has a resurrection in store for you too. Keep your thoughts on the Word of God day and night, and let it be what you speak. Do what is written, and put your confidence and your need for approval in the one who cannot fail.

It's interesting to me that Joshua's first assignment as Israel's newly appointed leader was to take them across the Jordan River (Joshua 3). When Israel first crossed through the parted waters of the Red Sea under Moses's command, it was a no-turning-back moment and a sign that the Lord was with Moses and would fight for them. Now, God established Joshua as their leader and exalted him in their sight through the same extraordinary miracle of parting the waters. They stood that day on solid, dry ground. Christ not only stood by him in every season, but He reconciled him and elevated him in the eyes of people.

Can I share something with you? God is not ashamed of you! Whether your pain was caused by a decision you made, by the hardships of life or by something someone did to you, God will walk unashamed by your side. Be honest in your observations of your own hurts and hang-ups and be honorable in your tone toward others, and you'll have a recipe for unshakable confidence. The Lord will defend you and rebuild what was once lost. He's not done with you, just as he was not done with Joshua—there is still leadership in you. If you are willing to step out in the waters of uncertainty, you can count on God to part them for you. However deep you feel in your insecurity, sin, past or problem, God's love for you is deeper still. He will not let you drown. He is with you every step of the way! *Be Confident.*

My Reflections

"When we lose one blessing,
another is often most
unexpectedly
given in its place."
-C.S. Lewis

For though the righteous
fall seven times, they rise
again, but the wicked stumble
when calamity strikes.
Proverbs 24:16 (NIV)

Chapter 6
Be Redeemed

It seems that with every year and after every kid, gravity tends to set in a little more. Please don't leave me hanging on this one (no pun intended!). Let me explain: I have a tattoo of a dolphin that I got as a teenager, then when I was pregnant, it turned into a whale, and after three kids, it is now a swordfish.

Seriously, though, if you're considering getting a tattoo, please think twice. My teenage self did not consider my post-childbirth self in making that decision. In fact, there are probably many things in my life that I wish I could have a do-over. How about you? Do you have anything you wish you could go back and do differently? I once asked this question in a prison I was *God will turn regrets into redemption!* ministering at, and the whole room raised their hands. Listen, we all have regrets and there's no magic time machine, but God wants to turn those regrets into redemption!

My hope is that with age, I will also obtain wisdom to make better decisions so I have fewer regrets, but we can probably all attest to the fact that age doesn't necessarily equate wisdom. In fact, I know some women that are sixty, but their social media outbursts sound more like a hormonal sixteen-year-old! There has to be a reason that Proverbs relates wisdom to a woman:

For wisdom is better than rubies, and all the things one may desire cannot be compared with her. Proverbs 8:11 (NKJV)

God wants to adorn His girls with wisdom, which is so much better than adorning our outside while we are dying on the inside. There should be benefits to aging, and I think redemption is one of them. To every reader who has made a regrettable mistake, I'm telling you, it can be redeemed. To redeem means to gain back or to regain something in exchange for payment.[11] We can regain things we've lost that have been stolen or that we gave away because we didn't see the value in them at the time.

Joshua and his people had lost time and time again. They spent four hundred years in slavery and then were led to the Promised Land, only to meet it with doubt. Then they had to spend forty more years in the desert paying for their forty-day bad report. Now, would they be up for the opportunity for redemption when it came to them?

In Joshua 2, we find their story of redemption. Redemption isn't generally a quick moment. It looks more like a journey and one that will pick up unlikely people along the way. You remember how Moses sent out twelve spies and only two came back with a good report? Well, we can learn from history, and we can also be jaded by history. I'm not sure which one Joshua was at this particular moment when they came up on the city of Jericho, but Joshua knew God was directing him to check it out, so he sent out some spies. You want to guess how many? You got it. Two!

When the spies arrived in Jericho, they entered the house of a prostitute named Rahab. Again, not sure whose idea that was; sounds like a recipe for disaster to me. The King gets wind of it and tells her to send them out, but instead, she hides them and lies for them. To their awe, not only does she save them, but she then gives them intel:

> *I know that the LORD has given you this land and that a great fear of you has fallen on us, so that all who live in this country are melting in fear because of you. We have heard how the LORD dried up the water of the Red Sea for you when you came out of Egypt, and what you did to Sihon and Og, the two kings of the Amorites east of the Jordan, whom you completely destroyed. When we heard of it, our hearts melted in fear and everyone's courage failed because of you, for the LORD your God is God in heaven above and on the earth below. Joshua 2:9-11 (NIV)*

Forty years prior to this moment, ten of the twelve spies had declared to all of Israel that they looked like "grasshoppers," aka small, in the eyes of their enemy. I can relate to how they felt, but that doesn't mean that was the truth. As women, we tend to look at our flaws and others' achievements and falsely compare our differences because we share the commonality of womanhood. It's like saying strawberries and tomatoes should both taste the same and be used in the same ways because they are both red and fruit. I do not want strawberry sauce on my spaghetti! That's why we are supposed to keep our eyes on Jesus to see ourselves as He sees us and rightfully step into our unique and distinct purposes! How will we ever unite to fight a real enemy when our eyes are never on the right target?

Rahab's words had to pierce the hearts of the spies as they thought of their fathers and mothers who had died in the wilderness because of their flawed view of themselves and the capability of their mighty God. All that time they had been so worried about how they looked to someone else, but their enemy didn't see them as they saw themselves. They didn't see them as small; instead, they saw the power of God on them and that all of Israel had been marked with God's protection and provision. When partnered with the Lord, we are not who we think we are!

> *When partnered with the Lord, we are not who we think we are!*

Take a moment to really accept that when you choose Christ as your Lord and Savior, you are marked by God for greatness. We will never commit to something we don't believe in. We can be convinced for a moment, but to actually have buy-in and invest, we have to have a deep belief that is birthed through a relationship. What do you believe about God? The Israelites forgot the power of God, and they mistakenly saw themselves as small. Eventually, this mistake was redeemed when their children encountered Rahab.

But what lie had Rahab believed for herself? Rahab believed in the God of Israel, but she coupled her belief in Him with fear for forty years because she didn't know the true character of God. She thought, "This God is the God of Israel who can part the seas . . . ," but she feared that all He had in store for her was a sea of death. What Rahab was fearful of was the very thing that God sent to free her. She saw death, but God saw redemption. You might be sitting here today seeing death and disappointment, but God sees freedom for you. He's parting the waters, and the very struggle that you are trying to run from just might be the thing God uses to show you the depth of His love.

My husband's cousin has a past that has most certainly defined his life. He made a very bad decision on a night full of high emotion. There were so many factors that completed this perfect storm. That night cost him. It cost his family. It cost people that he didn't even know at the time. Because of his decision, he is currently living out a life sentence in prison with a possible chance of parole. Every three years he has had the opportunity to go before the parole board, but each time, he has been denied. You think that would crush him after twenty plus years of incarceration, and each time it's hard for all of us that love him, but these are his words to us: "If I never get out, I'm free. Prison was the best thing that ever happened to me because this is where I met Jesus."

Like Rahab, many of us can see God's promise for everyone around us, but not for ourselves. Rahab thought God's plans were to harm her. She thought that God only had a promise and a hope for one type of person, "the chosen," but God said to her by His actions, "You are my chosen." You see, God is not just the God of Israel. He is the God who came that all (that includes you) who believe in Him will be saved (John 3:16). He wants to move your mountain. He wants to part the sea in front of you. He is here to be your pathway to your destiny in Christ. He will use your prison to set you free. Believe in Him and partner with Him.

So Rahab makes her plea to the spies to save not just herself but everyone in her household. When we dream, let's dream generationally! Let's not settle for small cookies. Let's plea for things that will change the trajectory of our lineage. She made her request, and the spies granted it, but with a few requirements that would be determining factors for her freedom on the coming doomsday. As Rahab let the spies down by a rope through her window, they gave her specific steps to follow if she truly wanted to experience the protection of God and accept her new place and new identity among the Israelites:

> *Now the men had said to her, "This oath you made us swear will not be binding on us unless, when we enter the land, you have tied this scarlet cord in the window through which you let us down, and unless you have brought your father and mother, your brothers and all your family into your house. If any of them go outside your house into the street, their blood will be on their own heads; we will not be responsible . . ." Joshua 2:17–19 (NIV)*

Rahab was also given some warnings. If you leave the house, you are out of God's protection, His covering, and that will cause you death. God wants you to thrive and live a prosperous life, but to go outside of His will means that you leave His protection. I wonder how many of us have tried to receive the promises of God outside of the house of God. I'm a preacher's kid so trust me, I get church hurt, but one thing I know is that the house of God has provided me safety, protection, and provision even through hurt and pain. I remember during my years of rebellion searching the world for peace and purpose, but I came up short. There is nothing that can compare to being in the house of God.

What did this mean for Rahab? She would have to let some relationships die, the places she used to hang out, the habits she once exercised and some thoughts she once embraced. Her whole community was going to look different. Her job would look different. She could no longer dress the same, speak the same or keep the same company. That can feel harsh, but God doesn't give us warnings to harm us or even to take the fun away but rather to protect us. God knew what was going to happen to that city and to Rahab if she chose to stay submerged in the culture she had grown up in. The city burned to the ground, but Rahab and her family were saved. She was redeemed.

Choosing Redemption

Action is always required for change to occur. My pastor often says, "Two-thirds of God's name is Go!" God will always give us the tools and opportunity to change but tells us the responsibility is now ours. You make the decision. You choose to read the Bible. You choose to pray. You choose to get up and go to church. You choose to forgive. You choose to get involved in the Christian community. It's all available to you, but you have to take that next step the Lord keeps speaking to you about. Jesus paid the price on the cross for our sins and for our freedom so that everything that is behind us can be redeemed. Now the responsibility to walk in it is ours.

Just like with a winning lotto ticket, they don't call you to tell you that you have won, you must get involved by watching, looking, listening, filing a claim, and then you will receive your prize. God is telling you to get involved: watch, look, listen, and go claim the prize that He has already purchased for you. Israel didn't claim their prize for forty years! Rahab said that as soon as the seas parted, they knew that their land belonged to the Israelites, but even God's people often don't claim all that God has for them. If the devil can't make you sin, he'll try to render you useless.

Israel had a decision, and they chose the forty-year route. Have you ever made a seven-day journey turn into forty years because you wouldn't follow instructions? Maybe you don't like to be told what to do or you struggle with doubt, fear, or maybe even pride or laziness has kept you from walking it out. God's asking you today how long will you wait. He has more for you than where you are at today. Repeat that to yourself: "God has more for me than where I am today."

Maybe you're feeling like those God-sized dreams have expired, and it's just too late. Possibly, you feel like you've lived too much life and those things you once wished for are impossible. Well, I've learned through my mother-in-law that expiration dates are really just suggestions. I've pulled out cans from her pantry that are more than a decade past the expiration date, but I better not dare be caught throwing them away! "It's still good," she tells me. Where I may disagree with her on my faith in those canned preservatives, I do believe that God has preserved some great things for you.

Letting Go of Your Past

Your past does not have to be the defining factor of your future. Have you ever known someone that has been through some stuff and everyone knows about it? You see them coming down the hall, and you turn to go in the opposite direction because you don't want to get stuck in a conversation with them. They are so bitter that they turn even the good things in their lives into negative ones because of their history. You can see it in their countenance. In contrast, I've known people that I have thought had a silver spoon their whole lives only to later find out the brutal life they've lived, but the redeeming power of God engulfed them and transformed them.

> *Your past does not have to be the defining factor of your future.*

God's desire for us is that we are so free from our past that people are shocked when they find out what we have really been through, not because we are not transparent, but because we are not defined by who we were or what we went through. We are defined by who Christ is in us! I think about my pastor who saw her dad die right in front of her own eyes as he was preaching when she was just nineteen years old. Then, she had cancer while she was pregnant with her first baby at twenty-three, and she lived on welfare and food stamps for the first three years of planting our church. All of that, but you would think by looking at her that she is just a Barbie doll who had this incredible life and has never struggled. What I've learned from her is the true nature of God's healing power! I've watched God redeem her emotional pain, physical body and financial disasters.

Now let's look at the conditions that were placed on Rahab's freedom. She was told to tie or bind the scarlet cord that she used to let the spies down her window. What do you think of when you think of scarlet? My mind immediately goes to the well-known book published in 1850 called *The Scarlet Letter: The Romance*, which centers on a woman who had an affair and was publicly humiliated by having to wear a scarlet letter *A* for the rest of her life so everyone would know what she did before they knew who she was.

Rahab was an adulterer by career. I wonder how she wound up as a prostitute. Was it a series of bad choices, or was it decided for her? Regardless of how she got there, I'm sure that she struggled with the thought that she would wear this affliction for the rest of her life. Do you ever feel that way, thinking that there's no hope for an escape?

It's the very thing that binds us that God will often use to give us an opportunity. God will always meet you right where you are. Those spies couldn't have hidden in just anyone's house. Men came and went from Rahab's house unnoticed all of the time. Often in scripture we can see symbolisms that help us to understand an even deeper revelation in the historical stories in the Bible.

Let's see how this works:

- ♥ The cord = Our past
- ♥ The color scarlet = The blood of Jesus
- ♥ The window = Transparency

If the scarlet cord represents Rahab's past life of adultery, watch what God says to do with it: *bind it!* God's telling you that same thing today. What's been taunting you from your past, bind it in the name of Jesus. When we ask God for forgiveness, He gives it to us. So take your past, bind it and put it in the window of your life, unashamed as a testimony of God's redemption. The very thing that bound you will now be on display for the glory of God, and it will be used as a tool for freedom for others.

Many of us are bound by the vicious attacks of the enemy. The enemy is known as the accuser, and in my life, he has certainly lived up to that name. Day and night he throws accusations around, reminding me of all my mistakes, telling me how I could have done better, seeding thoughts of how people are against me or tormenting me with every failure. I can listen to those lies and even nurture them, or I can use the authority I have through the forgiveness Jesus has given me and stand up to those thoughts. Do you know you don't have to listen to that trash anymore?

I remember a situation where I had to activate this revelation. One day I was driving home, and I was frustrated with my husband, so all these thoughts started to flood my mind of how he had hurt me and disappointed me in our marriage. I let the thoughts go on for about two minutes before I snapped out of the enemy's trap and realized what he was doing. Out loud, in my car, by myself, I began to rehearse the many amazing things that my husband had done for me and for our family. He is truly my best friend, but the enemy had just used a bad day and bad timing to try to get me to think otherwise. I prayed for him and blessed him. I couldn't wait to get home to him that day. I took authority to bind the enemy with the rope of remembrance! I saw the trap of a vain imagination and didn't stay in it. Now you can see the trap, and you no longer have to stay in a cycle of torment, pain and deprivation. God says He has given you the power through him to bind it. You are no longer subject to your past; it is now a tool, not torture.

When redeemed your past is a tool not torture.

Break the Cycle

This book is proof that our past is a tool. God's using everything behind me that once caused me shame to be useful to lead others to the healing power of Jesus. Rahab used her cord, which represents her past, to set the spies free, and then, ultimately, it was because she took the authority to bind it and expose it in the window of her life that she set her whole family free, redeeming all of them! There are generational things that God wants to see broken off of your family. But this won't just happen. You have to be a part of that freedom for your family.

As much as I have struggled with rejection in my life, I can now step back and see that it's been a negative generational influence in my family line. My great-grandfather was shot and killed in a drunken fight when my papaw was only seven years old. His dying wish was that a relative would raise my papaw, not his own mother. At such a young age, my papaw lost his dad, and he felt the effects of rejection through this death. In addition, his mom gave him away without a second thought. His aunt and uncle took him in and told him, "If you don't do what I tell you to do, I will break your plate and send you back across the river," meaning if he didn't work the farm, he wouldn't eat. That was the extent of love and affection that he had growing up.

My papaw longed for family and had his own, but having never experienced love, he didn't know how to give it. He was harsh, critical and never showed up to support my dad in sports. He didn't even go to his high school graduation and many other things throughout his growing up years left him feeling rejected. My dad grew up and loved the Lord, but in his own struggle for acceptance, he often sacrificed his family at the altar of ministry. He tried to find his approval through works, which is such a trap of the enemy because the enemy knows we can never do enough to earn the love of God. God already loves us fully. We do not have to earn it, we have to receive it. My dad is now one of my best friends and biggest supporters (as was his dad to him in his adult years), and he often reminds me to not make the same

God already loves us fully. We do not have to earn it, we have to receive it.

mistakes he did. I know that I'm not perfect in parenting, but one thing is for sure, this generational curse of rejection has been broken off my family.

Let me share with you a glimpse of how far removed my kids are from rejection. When my youngest daughter was in second grade, she went to camp for the first time. Her counselor asked her, "Do you think that your mom and dad are missing you right now?" She responded, "Oh yeah. They are missing me so much they are crying in their pillows!" OK, so we may have overcorrected, but our kids know beyond a shadow of a doubt that they are loved and accepted. As adults, each of us needs to know that no matter our earthly experience, we are loved and accepted by our heavenly Father.

The scriptures teach us that we can see our fathers sin but choose to go the other direction, and when we do, we will begin a generational blessing for our families (Exodus 20:6), and that's exactly what happened with my family. If you see a pattern in your lineage, know that you can be the change, and it can be redeemed. Sometimes the enemy puts fear in us that we won't know how to be a good parent because of the things we've experienced, but I say the complete opposite! If you went through some rough stuff, guess what? You are better equipped to handle the things that will try to come against your kids. You knew what you needed from your parents, so now you can recognize warning signs and give your kids exactly what you needed.

With generational fears, you can respond in one of two ways: embrace the same fears being passed down from generation to generation or do the hard things to break the cycle. That's what happened with Israel. One generation died in the wilderness, and the next generation declared that they would trust God and walk into the scary battles they had to face in order to receive victory.

Joshua led this victorious charge, but he too had to face a choice when he faced Jericho, his first battle as Israel's redemptive leader. Outside of the Jericho walls, by himself, left to his own thoughts, fears and even strategy, he encounters an angel:

> *Then the Commander of the Lord's army said to Joshua, "Take your sandal off your foot, for the place where you stand is holy." And Joshua did so. Joshua 5:15 (ESV)*

Something so special happened at that moment. Before Rahab would be redeemed inside of Jericho, Joshua was redeemed outside of the Jericho walls. In order to get the victory, he had to gain back the territory in his mind. Here's a little context for you: the custom in Israel concerning exchanging and redeeming of property was to take off one's sandal and give it to the other (Ruth 4:7).

There was a holy exchange that happened when Joshua took off his sandal because God was telling Joshua that he was redeeming his past, his pain, his time, his dreams, his reputation, his territory and the way he saw himself. You may see forty years of waste and disappointment, but what God sees is an opportunity for redemption. God is not in the business of erasing your

God is not in the business of erasing your past; He's in the business of redeeming it.

past; He's in the business of redeeming it. He uses it all to build.

Redemption doesn't get any better than that. You don't have to repeat the cycle. You get to choose.

Choose Differently

Choosing differently means change. I'm not too fond of change. I think it's because as women, we crave security. That kind of feels odd to say because I'm a little bit of a daredevil. I have been zip lining, I've killed a snake, I've been on mission trips and jumped out of an airplane! Still, I went home and had my same nightly routine after each of those adventures. I even carry my pillow with me wherever I travel because there's something comforting about putting my head down on the same pillow each night.

Choosing differently means change.

Rahab chose a different path for herself, but in order for her to walk in it, she had to make some major life changes. She surrounded herself with a totally different culture of people. People that she didn't necessarily have much in common with except for the fact that God had rescued them all! She chose to leave a city that she once knew, places she used to eat, all the familiar things. In doing so, she also got to leave behind a poor reputation. She got to die to the small, insignificant way she saw herself.

Check this out:

> *Salmon the father of Boaz, whose mother was Rahab,*
> *Boaz the father of Obed, whose mother was Ruth,*
> *Obed the father of Jesse,*
> *and Jesse the father of King David.*
> *David was the father of Solomon, whose mother had been*
> *Uriah's wife, . . .*
> *and Jacob the father of Joseph, the husband of Mary, and*
> *Mary was the mother of Jesus who is called the Messiah.*
> *Matthew 1:5-6,16 (NIV)*

Do you see this? Rahab, the prostitute, was in the lineage of Jesus Christ! Rahab changed her lineage in a big way. She changed what her kids would be a part of by putting her belief into action. All of Rahab's life she had just been living out what had been spoken over her, what she had been named. Rahab means Egypt and Egypt in the Bible represents lust (Ezekiel 16:26). As a prostitute, her living fully depended on the sexual desires of men. I don't know if she ever saw more for herself, but God did, and He interrupted her path with two men who were marked by God and not by lewd desires. Instead of being abused by men, she was protected and brought into a true community where she could build a loving family. God even redeemed her sexuality by giving her a husband, not a bunch of cheap thrills. He gave her a healed view of men, sex and God's very character and nature. For anyone that has been sexually abused or has a past of sexual sin, this should give you great peace and hope. She confessed her belief in God and she went to drastic lengths to turn from all she once knew. As a result,

God took her from the lowest of lows and placed her in royalty.

Let me tell you a story. At age thirteen a girl was given to a much older man when her step-dad lost a bet in a card game. She was made to live with him as his wife and experienced unimaginable abuse until she finally ran away. At sixteen, she gave birth to her first child. When her daughter turned sixteen years old, she also had a daughter whose father named her after the two women he was cheating on her mom with. He walked out of their lives when their daughter was only six months old. That girl grew up in a home where they didn't go to church, yet she would pray and find people to take her on Sundays. She fell in love and got married at sixteen to a godly man that was called to the ministry. She too had a daughter, and she was oh so careful about naming her with distinction. Her name meant heavenly angel, and she prayed every day over that little girl. That little girl grew up and married a godly man and went into the ministry, and she too became pregnant with a daughter. The doctors said that her daughter would have difficulties all her life, but her parents wouldn't receive that report over their baby. So they gave her a name meaning "my peace in the battle" (Is this starting to sound familiar?). She was born six weeks early. Two surgeries later the only reminder of her struggles are a few tiny scars the size of my pinky. As I shared earlier in this book, that little girl is my daughter. You see, my mom changed her lineage. She should have been a statistic. My sisters and I should be from a broken home with different fathers, abandoned and rejected, but God stepped in and gave a little girl a dream, and she rose up and lived a different life.

Your story, no matter how far removed, is a powerful weapon of warfare, not only to your family but to the kingdom of God, to the advancement of the church! It's not too late to have victory in your life. It was not too late for Rahab either. The same scarlet cord, representing her past, that was tied and put in Rahab's window to save her family was also used by the spies to climb out her window and down the city walls to safety. God's grace is big enough to overcome your history, to overcome the hand that you have been dealt. It's not too late to change the course of your family. God's grace is big enough to overcome your past and claim the promises He has for you. God doesn't look at you and see a mess. God looks at you and sees a daughter. He sees you as beautiful. Rahab was no longer called "Rahab the Prostitute." She was known as Rahab a mother, Rahab the ancestor of Jesus Christ.

Today you have a choice. Who will you be known as? What type of future will you leave for those you love? *Be redeemed.*

"Failure should be our teacher, not our undertaker. Failure is delay, not defeat. It is a temporary detour, not a dead end. Failure is something we can avoid only by saying nothing, doing nothing, and being nothing."

-Denis Waitley

Have I not commanded you? Be strong and courageous. Do not be afraid; do not be discouraged, for the Lord your God will be with you wherever you go.

Joshua 1:9 (NIV)

Chapter 7

Be Strong and Courageous

Have you ever noticed that with age, we tend to play it safe? How many times over the course of your childhood did you hear adults around you say, "Be careful?" I say that to my children all the time, but throughout scripture, believers are told a different message: be strong and courageous.

In Joshua 1, a new season is upon Israel because their beloved leader, Moses, has died. Three times in this chapter Joshua is told to be strong and courageous, twice by God, and the third time by the people who have devoted themselves to following his leadership. No one wants to follow an indecisive or fearful person, but that's exactly what we can become when we've been hurt or hindered in life. You can get to a place in your adulthood where you no longer feel strong or courageous; instead, you feel like a failure.

My life has been filled with times when I've felt like a failure. I have failed in motherhood, pastoring, marriage, finances, my profession, and my friendships—you name it, and I've failed it! In these moments of failure, the enemy wants to steal our confidence and leave us paralyzed in shame and fear, depleting us of all strength and courage. The enemy wants to make us fearful so that we won't do anything of significance.

Yet failure does not have to define us; it can actually help us. Failure as a mom has helped me to teach my kids how to apologize and live a transparent and honest life. Not too long ago, my teenage daughter called me out for zoning out all the time, especially when she was trying to talk to me about her day. It made me aware, and I apologized and took it as an opportunity to grow in that area of failure so I could value the relationships God has given me. I want to be present.

Failure in my marriage has helped me to be honest with how I feel. Instead of stuffing all those emotions down and exploding over socks on the floor, I can have a real adult conversation with my husband about my needs and what I'm going through. We didn't get it right those first few years, but as we grew, so did the strength of our marriage. We became more intimate because we were courageous enough to be honest about the big things and the little things.

Failure in our finances has taught me how to not just bring God my tithe but to trust Him fully as our provider! You can tithe and still not trust, so failure there has brought me to a new level of faith, as God has redeemed our time and money. Failure at work taught me how to get back up, not be a perfectionist and surround myself with people that are smarter than me. As you can see, failure has been one of the greatest successes in my life.

We can also feel depleted not through our own failure but from the failure of others not supporting us when we are standing up for the right things. Like Joshua, many of us have started our journey with strength in our convictions, but through the course of time, we have compromised our values because of the blows we've taken in the past when we chose to do the right thing. When you've had the courage to do what was right and then lost, that can impact you so deeply. Doing the right thing and then still losing hurts. I've lost in life, even when choosing the right things, the righteous things. I've lost money, friends, position . . . It hurts. I love that the scriptures tell us that God is just so we can count on Him to make wrongs right, but He's not just on my timeline and His justice doesn't always align with my vengeance.

Circling

I hate delays! My husband and I went to our local airport, which we frequent, and this time we circled. There was so much construction that was changing the landscape of the airport that we went around it three times and still missed the exit. Finally, after the fourth time of circling, we made it to the right entrance to the parking garage. We were so frustrated. It didn't matter that we had been there before, what mattered is that we knew the right way to navigate the road we were on that day.

Circling sucks! Do you agree? Have you found yourself circling the same mistakes, the same insecurities, the same financial battles, the same health crisis, the same relational issues, the same triggers and you're just done? Good! Let's be done, not with the road God has us on but with our way of navigating it. Let's not insert assumptions into familiar roads that altogether need new piloting.

I'm sure Joshua faced many circular conversations in his head as he began to step into familiar paths of leadership. When God said, "Be strong and courageous," He was speaking directly to those conversations that might have gone something like "What if. . . . What if it happens again . . . What if I fail . . . What if God doesn't do it . . . What if I'm not the leader that they think I am. . . . What if they really stone me this time?" We can't and shouldn't determine truth by the thoughts in our heads. We determine truth solely by the unchanging Word of God!

Along with the "what if" game, we often play the blame game. Joshua is now in charge, so he can't blame the people because he's now their leader. He can't blame Moses; he's dead. He can't blame God, because God said that He would be with him and He gave Joshua all authority to take the land. What blame game do you play? It's time to step up to the plate. It's now your time to stop rehearsing the past and step up to lead. We can circle all we want to on what-ifs and blame, and some of us want to, not because it isn't annoying but because it's familiar. We can get very comfortable in the familiarity of our dysfunction if we allow ourselves to. Challenge yourself now to break the cycle. Don't stay in history, make history!

History or History Maker

Picking up the story in Joshua 5:13, we read: "It came to pass, when Joshua was by Jericho, that he lifted his eyes and looked" (ESV).

Don't stay in history, make history!

Facing Jericho I can imagine that it seemed as though the walls had gotten even bigger and stronger. Before, when Joshua was a spy, he had stood with no fear. The scripture recalls Joshua as being bold, courageous, a warrior, but now, now he's forty years older and has a new challenge called history. You see, he knew the last time he stepped out with great courage things didn't go as he had planned. He had walls that he was facing not only physically, but now he also had walls that had been building for the last forty years in his heart and mind—walls of insecurity, rejection, doubt and fear.

For forty years, he walked with people that once wanted to stone him. I'm sure there were times of humiliation and rejection, but the path to a miraculous resurrection is paved with rejection. Jesus understands being righteous, standing for the right things, and feeling forsaken, yet his identity remained secured from the cross to grave to resurrection. Not even the tomb could hold Christ down because the source of His power was not the acceptance of people, it was the acceptance of the Father.

The path to a miraculous resurrection is paved with rejection.

If Joshua lifted his eyes, that means that at one point they were shut or downcast, which suggests his strength and courage were failing. Eyes speak to vision. My father-in-law wasn't blind all of his life, but because of his disease, his eyes gradually grew dimmer and dimmer until he could no longer see at all. I believe we can be infected with a disease called fear when we are

Failure either becomes you or drives you to become!

exposed to something called failure. Failure either drives you to become better, or it attaches itself to you as your identity.

We can recognize the warning signs of a failure mindset by thoughts like:

- ♥ I'll never be more than this.
- ♥ This is all God has for me.
- ♥ I don't deserve good things.
- ♥ I'm being punished for my past.
- ♥ Why should I even try?

These notions bring to us a settling spirit that cripples and blinds our capacity for more.

What do you see in your life?

- ♥ Failure or future?
- ♥ Mistakes or possibilities?
- ♥ Lack or plenty?
- ♥ Mountains or miracles?

Friend, when we set our eyes on Jesus, who is our example, we become more and more like Him: righteous, confident, bold, peaceful, victorious. In doing so, we can be courageous in the face of failure. If we choose to see what God sees, we will have the courage to live without limitations. You are not who you think you are. You are not a failure; you are a success waiting to happen!

Joshua is caught in his mental battle between history and making history!

And behold, a man stood opposite him with his sword drawn in his hand. And Joshua went to him and said to him, "Are you for us or for our adversaries?" So he said, "No, but as commander of the army of the Lord I have now come."
Joshua 5:13-14 (ESV)

We can think we are all alone facing problems, but a war is being fought in the spiritual realm even as we speak right now because the enemy is after not just us but the future generations we represent. He's after our influence! Whether you think so or not, you are influencing people. The angels of God's army are fighting on your behalf here and now, just as they did for Israel, because a generational blessing awaits us when we say yes to Jesus! Joshua looked up and saw right past his natural problem and abilities, and he looked straight to a supernatural answer: seeing the invisible produces courage for the impossible.

Seeing the invisible produces courage for the impossible.

The angel of the Lord encamps around those who fear him, and he delivers them.
Psalm 34:7 (NIV)

I think each of us has experienced darkness in some form (shame, discouragement, abuse, oppression, depression, disappointment, sickness). It may have been a battle to just pick up this book today! We can be intimidated by evil in this world, be deceived by the lies of the enemy and manipulated by the schemes of darkness; or we can have the courage to believe the truth that every dark power is subject to the name of Jesus Christ. No other name is greater than the name of Jesus. It's the only name by which time is demarcated. It's the only name by which healings and miracles are given. All of heaven and earth are subject to the name of Jesus. It's the name above all names, the name by which we are saved, and we know that every knee will bow and every tongue will confess that Jesus Christ is Lord of all (Philippians 2:9-11).

In addition to these dark experiences, we can feel the overwhelming boast of the enemy through the constant stream of bad news, whether that be listening to our TV, turning on a podcast, talking with a neighbor or reading an article. Remember there are more for us than against us! One-third of the angels left heaven to follow Satan's boisterous claims of superiority to Jesus, but the scriptures tell us that Satan and his new following fell like lightning. There wasn't some long, drawn-out battle. It was done just like that. Two-thirds of the Lord's army is still at work and in operation of His command today. In fact, in Psalm 91, we are reminded that God orders His angels to protect us wherever we go. Joshua was strengthened when he saw the angel of the Lord, knowing that God was on his side. His courage could be built by remembering God's promises for all of Israel. He didn't have to rehearse the pain of the past, but he could choose to remember the miracles of the past. He knew in his heart of hearts that God was for him and no one could thwart the strength or will of God. We too can draw strength and courage from the knowledge that painful experiences can lead to miraculous moments.

Worship

When I'm facing hard moments and just don't know where to go or what to do, worship becomes my place of strength and courage. Joshua and I are alike in this way, as the scriptures say *"he fell on his face to the earth and worshiped" Joshua 5:14 (ESV)*.

Here he was facing a city, not having his mentor to give him direction or clarity on the next step and all of the pressure was on him. He had heard from God before, and he needed to hear from God again. The city of Jericho was often associated with the word for smell, so we can assume it was because of the pleasant fragrances of the fruits and spices which grew there.[12] Worship is our pleasing aroma that we send to heaven when giving praise to God. Joshua knew that his worship to God would bring a fresh scent to heaven and begin a beautiful conversation of direction, encouragement and support.

My husband loves cologne. Some people are wine connoisseurs, but he is a fragrance connoisseur. He can tell you exactly what the core ingredient of a scent is just by taking one big sniff. One morning I walked in on him in the bathroom getting ready for work. He strutted up to his cabinet, with all his colognes perfectly lined up, threw his shoulders back and said, "What kind of man am I today?" as he chose the perfect fragrance to match his mood!

Our moods matter. Our moods determine the worship we will give and to whom we will give it. We can worship darkness just as easily as we can worship Christ, maybe even easier. It's not hard to look at all the things stacked against us. You'll know whom you are worshiping by the ingredient you are worshiping with. The core ingredient to worshiping darkness is fear; it's an awful smell! Even animals can smell fear. Fear says I don't believe what God said is true, I believe the lies of the enemy, I believe the bad report, I believe the "no" over the dream. However, the core ingredient to pure, holy worship is obedience, which produces the courage and strength to fearlessly proclaim, "I trust God no matter what!"

Joshua fell on his face to turn his heart back to a place of pure worship. We give God our best worship in times of pain, in the unknown and in waiting. When we worship through pain and disappointment without knowing or understanding what God will do next, we prove our faith in Him. When we do this, we send a pleasing aroma to the nostrils of heaven. God looks on us during these times and says boastfully, like a proud papa, "Do you see that worship? That's my girl! She doesn't know what I'm about to do, but see how she trusts me?" When you're faced with a wall of a problem, turn your face toward God. He will not disappoint you.

When you're faced with a wall of a problem, turn your face toward God.

Joshua fell on his face so he wouldn't experience the pain of failure but would gain the strength of praise. In response to our worship, God gives us His full attention. Be ready to listen to what the Lord wants to say when we bring our prayers to Him. Too often in prayer, we do all of the talking, but if you will just be still, the Lord is speaking and He wants to impart a word to you that will give you strength in the wait. Let's learn from Joshua and his question to the messenger from the Lord: *"What does my Lord say to His servant?" Joshua 5:14 (ESV)*

By asking this question, Joshua was saying, I'm ready and willing to do whatever you ask. His courage was fueled up for the task at hand, and it's a good thing that it was because his faith was going to be stretched for this one. Why does God never choose the obvious route? He has the most experienced warrior in Joshua and instead of utilizing that strength, these are His instructions:

March around the city once with all the armed men. Do this for six days. Have seven priests carry trumpets of rams' horns in front of the ark. On the seventh day, march around the city seven times, with the priests blowing the trumpets. When you hear them sound a long blast on the trumpets, have the whole army give a loud shout; then the wall of the city will collapse and the army will go up, everyone straight in. Joshua 6:3-5 (NIV)

And just like that, he was circling again. I would have loved to have some reality TV around this whole experience. I wonder what Rahab was thinking inside of the Jericho walls. I wonder if they were being mocked or ridiculed as they silently circled. I wonder if anyone hurled anything at them over the wall or if the city was planning an attack of their own. We know nothing *except* when the trumpet sounded on that seventh day, the Israelites gave a shout of praise to God that crushed the walls of Jericho! Joshua wasn't circling without purpose! Nothing like this had ever happened before or has happened since. I pray my courage produces the type of faith to keep on circling when God tells me to stay committed to His plan. I want God to do things in my life that are outrageous and unbelievable!

Strength for Others

God does not waste moments of weakness in our lives, instead He uses them to build strength for others.

God arms me with strength, and he makes my way perfect.
Psalm 18:32 (NLT)

Fourteen years after my daughter was born, some friends of ours, like me, had their baby six weeks early. She too had to leave the hospital without her baby. Like me, she hadn't even had a baby shower and nothing went as planned, but who do you think was in that NICU with her? Who else could impart strength to her through our healing story? Who could relate to her and the moments of weakness felt? Me! In this moment, I had the opportunity to share that although she might feel like this was the worst day of her life, God was working on a testimony for her son. I declared God's goodness over their son that, like my Syrena, her son would know all his life that no weapon formed against him can prosper! I had faced a wall of a problem fourteen years earlier, I felt like a failure of a mother too weak to give my daughter what she needed, but now those same bricks, which were torn down by the healing power of Christ, were being used to build a pathway to healing and strength for others.

Have I not commanded you? Be strong and courageous. Do not be afraid; do not be discouraged, for the Lord your God will be with you wherever you go.
Joshua 1:9 (NIV)

Joshua did not courageously face a wall of a problem just for his own life, he faced it for others. Our lives, our pain and our decisions to be strong and courageous radically shape victory or defeat for others. All of Israel got to share in the victory at Jericho because Joshua didn't cower when it was his chance to step up and lead. He allowed his history to inform him, not to conform him. His courage gave strength to the army of Israel to now take the land their parents once feared. They circled for the last time!

Allow your history to inform you, not conform you.

Be of good courage. People need you to get back up and face that wall. You may think that your God-dream has expired, but let me remind you Joshua was close to eighty years old when he faced Jericho! There's still leadership in you. God is speaking to you today to let you know that as long as there's breath in your lungs, you can get up and take the land! Be strong and courageous. Don't try to "do" strong and courageous or just put it on for a moment, but *be* it, live it!

Jesus authored a plan of redemption for us on the cross through the bravest act in history so that we could face all adversity with strength and courage with Him by our side.

Fix the battle in your mind by fixing your eyes on Jesus.

Your plan may have failed, but God's plan never does! That day facing Jericho, Joshua got the victory before he ever got the victory. God fixed the battle in his mind because Joshua fixed his eyes on Jesus. He made some history so wild that we are still reading about it today. The choice is yours. Will you stay in history or be a history maker? *Be strong and courageous!*

My Reflections

"Be bold. If you're going to make an error, make a doozy, and don't be afraid to hit the ball."

-Billie Jean King

The wicked flee when no one pursues, but the righteous are bold as a lion.

Proverbs 28:1 (ESV)

Chapter 8
Be Bold

Being strong and courageous helps us deal with and grow from our failures, while being bold helps us face our fears head-on. In some ways, I'm pretty gutsy. Growing up we lived in some pretty rough places. It wasn't uncommon for someone that was drunk to stumble across our driveway or for suspicious activity to be happening in the alleyway behind our small, two-bedroom, one-bathroom house. Because of the rough neighborhoods we lived in, I was constantly on guard, aware of my surroundings for whatever encounter I might face. Our church often experienced break-ins and theft. At twelve, I stopped a boy much bigger than me from breaking into the church. Even though he tried to push me around, a boldness and authority came over me, and he ran. Two times, as a teenager, I saved my little sister from being abducted from our unfenced "backyard" as she was playfully unaware. I may be small, but I've always had to be mighty in my posture, operating in boldness to defend those I fiercely love. There's an authority I've unknowingly carried that when used, the enemy had to retreat.

Then there are other parts of my life that feel in complete contrast to the warrior others have seen. In 2019, I was getting ready to take my annual trip to Mozambique, Africa, to host our church's women's conference. I had been many times before, and I've never struggled with having the strength and courage to go to a foreign place, but there was something more, something special that I was sensing that God wanted to do this time around. I knew that whatever "more" was, it wouldn't be the usual planning or posture that would get us the desired goal; instead, it would take boldness.

The only way I knew to receive boldness of any kind was through prayer. Prayer has gotten me through so many tough moments of life. It has been my place of refuge and my place of encouragement to do the hard things, to step out and to stand up. It's important to have people in your corner that can pray for you, pray things off of you, and pray you up. I, of course, went straight to my pastor, knowing that she would have just the right words and connection with the Lord to help me on this assignment.

She first asked me, "What exactly do you want me to pray for?" I told her that I felt like God wanted to do something unique on our trip, something we hadn't experienced before. Since the area that we go into in Mozambique is the capital for witchcraft training, we would often encounter very dark things, but we would also see women released from tormenting spirits as they would give their lives to Christ and profess their faith publicly through water baptism. This year, I had specifically felt like God was asking me to have an opportunity for women to renounce witchcraft completely by burning any ceremonial cloths that would be used in ancestral worship, and through their choice to do that, God would perform miracles.

So I shared with her these things and asked her if she would specifically pray for me to be bold so I could do what God had asked me to do. She began to pray and said so confidently, "Lord, I don't know how this girl could get any more bold than she already is, but she's asked for it, so give it to her!" Wow. It's amazing how people see you versus how you see yourself. When I left that day, I began to pray all the way to my car. "Lord, what is she talking about? I don't feel bold." The key word here is *feel*. I distinctly heard the Lord say, "That's because boldness is not a feeling, it's a resolve." That was a mic drop moment in my life.

Fear is a feeling, but boldness is a resolve to do what God has called you to do no matter how you feel.

Fear is a feeling, but boldness is a resolve to do what God has called you to do no matter how you feel.

What triggers fear to rear its ugly head in your life and how do you face it? I have a host of unhealthy ways I've dealt with fear in my life: I've stayed up all night worried. I've been so anxious that it would manifest itself through stomach pains, stealing my appetite. I've hidden it in overcompensating tones that would say things like:

- ♥ It's no big deal.

- ♥ I didn't want it anyway.

- ♥ You can't hurt me.

- ♥ I've got thick skin.

- ♥ I don't need anybody.

- ♥ I wouldn't have been able to go even if they had invited me.

Additionally, I've been so afraid to do things, but I was more fearful of what people would think of me if I didn't follow through, so I did them while being scared. I feared the loss of reputation more than the deed itself.

Maybe that's why I wouldn't back down from a fight or why people would just assume I was OK instead of reaching out to me during times of change, heartache or devastation. I remember when I moved out to go to college, I had an expectation that my parents would miss me and show it by sending me care packages. When my older sister moved out, she received care packages with her favorite goodies, notes and money—things every college student needs. It set the bar for my expectations. I checked the mail with anticipation, and within the first two weeks, I had a letter from my dad. I excitedly opened the envelope only to discover a folded-up phone bill with charges highlighted in bright yellow and a yellow sticky note on top saying, "See the highlighted charges. You owe me a total of X dollars. Love, Dad." Oh, the days of long-distance boyfriends!

I was heartbroken again. Unmet expectations reinforced my feelings that I was not loved or wanted. After a year of being off on my own, I got up enough boldness to talk to my mom about some of my disappointments. I asked my mom, "Why didn't you ever call or do anything to show me you cared?" My mom replied, "I just thought you were OK. You've always been so strong and independent that I didn't think you needed us." Sometimes we put up a big front to protect our reputations and prove we are tough, but all we do is open the door for deeper hurt. We build walls to protect ourselves, but they keep us locked away and untouchable to relationships that could bring us life. This type of response to fear makes us hard as mud and sour as lemons.

However, we have the power to change. A year later, I made a move and had to start from scratch. I didn't think too much about it, because like my mom said, I've always been able to take care of myself. I'm a hard worker, so no matter where I was employed, I was promoted and was never lacking for opportunities. But it did not happen that way this time. There was no work and no opportunity. I was in a little apartment in downtown Austin, and for the first time ever, I didn't have a job, money or savings. I had never been in this position before and didn't know what to do, so I did the only thing I could do: I swallowed my pride and called my dad. I cried and felt so defeated. Not even a week later, I got a letter in the mail. I took a deep breath as I opened it. In that envelope my dad sent me a check to pay my rent for the month, and on top of his generosity, he added an extra $100 and said this was my "make it happen" money because he knew I could make it happen.

I was fearful to expose my hurt, but when I did, not only was I accepted but I was also supported and encouraged. This was one of the many heroic acts of my dad and a redeeming moment in our relationship. He was there for me. He provided for me. He was a good father. Sounds a lot like our heavenly Father to me. Fear once kept me silent in times of need, but now boldness in an act of humility gave me the space to see my father differently, and it afforded me the opportunity to get back on my feet.

Each of us responds differently to the feeling of fear, but we can all agree on one thing: fear is tormenting. When we experience it, we must face it in order to overcome it. My oldest daughter had the hardest time wanting to drive, the thought of it alone would send her into a panic attack. The only way to overcome her fear of the road was to make her drive. We had many meltdown moments in the car. Yet, she learned to drive and obtaining her license wasn't stolen from her by the bully of fear. Now, I must say that I thank God for the bright yellow magnet that says "student driver" that I would put on my bumper. I'm super appreciative to all my fellow Texas drivers that kindly refrained from honking and went around us as Syrena faced her fears. Today, I want you to go on a "facing my fear" road trip too.

Good Fear

Is there such a thing as good fear? Yes, fear isn't all bad in the right context. Fear is a feeling that we should listen to because it can indicate important things to us. There are sensible fears that keep us from running into a road full of traffic, putting our hands in fire or grabbing a hornet's nest. These are all good fears, don't you think? We should have some sense about ourselves to stay out of harm's way when we can. Let's think about risk versus reward before we make rash decisions that truly impact our lives. These good fears keep us safe, but for a moment, let's talk about another good fear that keeps us holy.

Scripture teaches us that we should have a reverent fear of the Lord.

The fear of the Lord is the beginning of wisdom.
Proverbs 9:10 (NIV)

Like a good father, He wants us to be alert and aware when a behavior is destructive to us or others. When we choose to make Jesus our Lord and Savior, our lives are no longer our own, which means His house, His rules. In my youth, I was afraid to show up at my house after curfew; likewise, we should have a reverent fear of God to follow His commands, which were given to provide us with safety. We will receive corrections because God wants us to live our best lives. A reverent fear of the Lord keeps us from compromising by guiding every decision we make through God's view on the matter.

Too many "Christians" today put more value on their own thoughts and ways than on God's thoughts and ways. We allow popular culture and catchphrases to inform our beliefs on gender, sexuality, abortion, marriage, modesty and more. This is a signal to us that we have lost the fear of God and therefore forfeit wisdom. God knew that Joshua would be faced with many opportunities to accept the fear and ways of the world instead of being bold in the face of adversity. Here are God's words of caution to Joshua:

Be careful to obey all the law my servant Moses gave you; do not turn from it to the right or to the left, that you may be successful wherever you go. Keep this Book of the Law always on your lips; meditate on it day and night, so that you may be careful to do everything written in it. Then you will be prosperous and successful. Joshua 1:7-8 (NIV)

God's desire for us is to be prosperous and successful and we can if we have a reverent fear of God submitting to His ways indicated in His Word. When we give in to the desires of our heart instead of recognizing that the heart is deceitful and wicked (Jeremiah 17:9), we lose (more about this in the next chapter). We live in the day of participation awards and treat our faith in the same manner, but the scripture tells us something completely different.

Not everyone who says to Me, "Lord, Lord," shall enter the kingdom of heaven, but he who does the will of My Father in heaven. Many will say to Me in that day, "Lord, Lord, have we not prophesied in Your name, cast out demons in Your name, and done many wonders in Your name?" And then I will declare to them, "I never knew you; depart from Me, you who practice lawlessness!" Matthew 7:21-23 (NKJV)

I want to be bold in my faith even if that means someone unfollows me. I want God to correct me even if it offends me because I want to truly know Him and I want Him to know me! I want Jesus to call me by name the day I meet Him face to face. David pens it so well in Psalm 23 when he likens the Father's correction to a rod and staff. He says, "They comfort me." Think about it, the rod and staff were used by the shepherd to strike the sheep. He would take the hook that is found on the end of the staff to guide the sheep that are separating from the flock back into the fold. It might hurt or be uncomfortable for a moment, but at the end of the day, the good Shepherd desires us to be led to green pastures and living water, not wander off to be eaten by prey or fall off a cliff.

I have many friends that have chosen abortion or been forced into aborting their babies, and what followed was many years of pain. None of which the world shared with them in their decision-making process. The pain was not from the rejection or condemnation of our church, our church was and is open-armed and accepting to all that want to know Jesus, rather the pain came from the damaging lies the enemy told them. Fear drove the decision, but that decision drove them to unnecessary pain. Now, they fight for life because they know the value of what they lost.

Let's not lose the fear of God for a hashtag. The enemy is baiting you with empty words, but God gives us the words of life even when they are hard to hear.

But Jesus, knowing in himself that his disciples were grumbling about this, said to them, "Do you take offense at this? . . . It is the Spirit who gives life; the flesh is no help at all. The words that I have spoken to you are spirit and life. But there are some of you who do not believe." . . . After this many of his disciples turned back and no longer walked with him.
John 6:61,63-64,66 (ESV)

Good fear keeps us moving in step with the Lord, boldly declaring His Word despite the conflicting views of our culture. Remember that God wants us to prosper so even when His opinion on the matter at hand conflicts with yours, He's not telling you to harm you, He's telling you to save you.

Irrational Fears

Then we have the fears that will literally make you go crazy. These fears are called irrational fears. Have you ever noticed how much the elderly talk about going to the bathroom? One woman up in years would share with me her bathroom issues every time we talked. I finally asked someone, "What's up with her obsession with the bathroom?" She had apparently had an irrational fear of having to get a colonoscopy bag. No matter how often she was assured that no doctor would ever do that to her over a day between movements, she would still face this fear daily. In the midst of COVID-19, she would continually have people take her to the emergency room because she was irregular.

Finally, after scheduling a few tests to make sure everything in her system was working properly (and it was), the doctor came in and said, "You are perfectly healthy for a woman your age. Stop going to the ER. You are putting yourself in more danger going to the ER when COVID is so high and there's absolutely nothing wrong with you."

At times, I think we too can be so constipated by fears that are putting us at risk, not because of any disease but because of our choice to be consumed by the wrong things. This poor woman had been so consumed with this irrational fear that the night before the appointment, she yelled out in the middle of the night with stomach pain. When she was checked on, they heard her stomach growl from hunger pains. She had been so afraid that she was barely eating, and even when she did eat, she would only eat an egg. She was starving herself to death; that's why her stomach hurt. After the appointment, she felt amazing and was at peace because the tests had come back negative. Nothing changed in her body, but everything changed in her mind. Now she could eat, laugh and sleep. The next few days she feasted.

What are you starving in your life because of irrational fears? Ponder that for a minute. Fear kept me from being the lead volunteer teacher in our three-year-old classroom at my church because I was afraid to read out loud, even in front of three-year-olds. Fear kept me from ever raising my hand in school. Fear kept me from applying to colleges. Fear kept me from trusting people. Fear starves our potential! Fear is a smoke screen that grabs your attention and distracts you from the truth.

Fear starves our potential!

Fear that Intimidates

When you turn forty, you get to do so many fun things, like have a mammogram. There's just nothing like your female parts getting squished all while having to remain dreadfully still to say, welcome to forty! If you've never had one, you really have something to look forward to. For me, it was just another thing to check off of the list of things I needed to get done. I wasn't expecting anything and maybe that's why I was in a bit of shock when I got a call back from the doctor. There was a place of "concern" on my left breast that warranted the call. They requested that I go to a specialist for better images through a more detailed mammogram and an ultrasound. I hung up the phone and had a quick cry before calling my husband.

Why do we often go straight to the worst-case scenario? Have you ever noticed how quickly we can go dark? My husband immediately started googling to see how common it was for you to get called back in. To be honest, I really tried hard to not allow my mind to go there. Google will not guard you. It will guarantee relentless calamity, stealing all your time and attention. Why don't you and I make a pact: let's be women that run to God, not Google!

Let's be women that run to God, not Google!

After I got off the phone with my husband, this was my prayer, "God, if there's nothing in my body, I want to thank you for my continued health. If there's something here that shouldn't be, let me glorify you in the process of my healing. This body is not my own and this earth is not my home."

Then I had to wait for my appointment. When there's a distance between where you are and where you want to be, the enemy wants to own that space by filling it with anxiety, fear, doubt, anger, worry, angst, isolation and sleepless nights, but as believers, we don't give the enemy the opportunity for a foothold in our lives. We are to immediately fill that space with prayer, with the Word of God, with a community of other believers and with worship. We are to prophesy over our situation and trust it in the hands of the one that can actually do something about it. There's a praise that is so pure and holy that we can only offer God in the wait, in the not knowing, saying to him, "God, even if I have to walk through this, you're still good, and I know you'll be good to me in it."

I was determined to make my wait matter. On the day of my appointment, my husband picked me up, and I said let's grab a bite to eat on the way. I was calm because I wasn't filled with anxiety or fear. He asked me, "How are you doing?" I was honest with where I was and told him, "I just want to get it done and know one way or the other so I can move forward." I went in, and after the mammogram, they said, "It's looking good." Then the ultrasound started and the nurse said she didn't see anything, but she wanted the doctor to confirm. Then the doctor came in and said, "What we saw before, we can't see today. You are cleared." It was a joyful ride home, to say the least!

Headspace

I was so happy about the diagnosis, but the miracle is not what happened in my body. There was likely nothing there to begin with and I thanked God for continued health. The miracle is what happened in my head. As believers we have to get our headspace straight! It's important for us to get the victory before we get the victory, just like Joshua did outside the Jericho walls.

Instead of spending that time waiting in fear and having every prayer I prayed focused on something that might not even exist, I was able to be present with my family, friends and work and make each day matter. I slept. I ate. I laughed. I smiled. I shared. I gave. A fearful Christian is a useless Christian. This is not to say that we shouldn't ever feel fear, but that we should not allow ourselves to be moved, bossed around, intimidated, distracted or paralyzed because of it.

A fearful Christian is a useless Christian.

Please do not hear a condemning tone from me, but one that encourages you to not allow the enemy to get you into a chokehold, rendering you useless. The longer the delay in our situation, diagnosis or healing, the more space the enemy has to afflict us with fear. Make a battle plan now on how you will live in those spaces we will all likely have to face. It's not that you won't have bad days in the delay, but you don't set up camp there. If we are aware of the schemes of the enemy, we don't have to fall victim to his tactics. God will frustrate the enemy's plan by revealing to us what he is doing, so even if our bodies begin to tremble and our minds begin to run, our spirit can say, "Hold on. Believe the Word of God!"

Here are God's unapologetic words to Joshua on how to face fear:

Have I not commanded you? Be strong and courageous.
Do not be afraid; *do not be discouraged, for the Lord your*
God will be with you wherever you go. Joshua 1:9 (NIV)

One of my dear friends battled for eight years with cancer
before she went home to be with Jesus at thirty-four years old.
I saw her on her worst days be grateful, lead worship, find
ways to serve the church from home and let people into her
most vulnerable moments. Her last couple of days in ICU,
when she should have been ridden in fear, she was worshiping
in faith. None of us are promised tomorrow, and there's not a
diagnosis that changes the fact that today is the day that
matters, so how will you choose to live in the space you are in?

When fear rules our head space, our conversations are circular.
Israel knew this truth all too well. They circled for forty years
because of fear, and they died in the wilderness they wandered
in. Fearful living is not God's plan or design for you. It's the
enemy that wants you to wander in fear, causing a life of
anxiety.

Where I've made strides forward, I can still see times when
fear overshadows the love that God has for me.

There is no fear in love. But perfect love drives
out fear, because fear has to do with punishment.
The one who fears is not made perfect in love.
1 John 4:18 (NIV)

God is not punishing you. Maybe you need to hear that today.
God loves you dearly and calls you his very own (1 Peter 2:9).
There is no fear in love! That's a statement that has power.

What we know from scripture is that Jesus is love, and He *so* loved us that He gave His life for us (John 3:16). If we find ourselves ridden with fear in an area of life, that is a reflection of a place that needs to experience the love of Jesus poured all over it. In that area, we can work on getting in the right headspace by embracing the love of Christ. It's a condemning thought to think the opposite of fear is faith because we are then ridden with the overthinking of how we have failed in faith, inciting more fear. Instead, we can embrace the truth of God's Word, understanding that fear cannot coexist with God's love. Furthermore, the love of God is not earned, it is received.

When battling fear, we can invite the love of God into our specific situation. Here are a few things you need to know about God's love for us that is declared in 1 Corinthians 13:4-12, which will help you respond to fear in a different way:

The character of Love:

- ♥ Love is patient.
- ♥ Love is kind.
- ♥ Love does not envy.
- ♥ Love does not boast.
- ♥ Love is not proud.
- ♥ Love does not dishonor others.
- ♥ Love is not self-seeking.
- ♥ Love is not easily angered.

- Love keeps no record of wrongs.
- Love does not delight in evil but rejoices with the truth.
- Love always protects.
- Love always trusts.
- Love always hopes.
- Love always perseveres.
- Love never fails.
- Love is greater than faith and hope.

In contrast, let's explore the lies fear tells us:

- Nothing is happening, so you need to make it happen on your own.
- God is angry with you.
- Everyone else's life is better than yours.
- You can only rely on you.
- You don't need help, no one would understand.
- God wants to humiliate you.
- You're selfish.
- You are too much.
- You are not forgiven.
- You can't handle the truth.
- You are exposed.
- God's plans for you are not good.
- Don't get your hopes up.

- ♥ Give up, there's no use.
- ♥ You're going to be disappointed.
- ♥ You don't have enough faith to be healed.

It's time to distinguish what and who Love is versus what fear is telling you. Only you can put an end to circular conversations by speaking the truth of who Jesus is in your situation. Do not engage with the enemy based on the fear that he is breathing down your throat! Get in the headspace of love.

When you do this, you will still face hardships, but you can do it without fear. At church one Sunday, one of our leaders came to me to ask for prayer. She had just been diagnosed with cancer. Tears streamed down her face as she shared with me the news. She told me, "I believe in God for a complete healing. In the meantime, God will use this to bring other people to Him, and I'm excited about that part." She was full of the love of God. She still cried as she would still experience hardship and pain, but she invited the Lord into it with her! She received God's love by pouring His Word into every corner of her life.

Boldness is not a bully bossing its way around with no concern for the fragile spaces it must often enter. Boldness affords us the tears in the trials, but it also wipes them away with the washing of the Word and moves us forward in the face of fear. God is well acquainted with our grief, and He is gentle with us

Boldness is not a bully bossing its way around with no concern for the fragile spaces it must often enter.

(Isaiah 53:3). When this beautiful sister shared her story with me, I thought, "I don't ever want to stop living until I stop living. With every last breath in me, I want to praise the Lord. I want to love as He loves."

Prayers that Matter

I have had a heart for Africa since I was a little girl. Even at seven and eight years old, I would share my burden for the continent with my mom. At times I would be so moved with concern, she would send me to my room with tissues and tell me to go pray. I would kneel by my bed, and I would cry out to the Lord. Who does that at such a young age? I didn't even know what to pray for; nevertheless, I prayed.

Looking back over all the years I have ministered in Africa, I often wondered if I'm reaping the harvest of prayers I prayed in my childhood years. I don't know if I was bold then, but my heart was pure and my trust was complete.

Trust is easy when you're little. I have heard that up until the age of eight, our belief systems are still being developed, so we really look to people around us to shape those beliefs. As we get older, we quickly learn a harsh life lesson: disappointment. Disappointment is so cruel; it takes the purity out of our adolescence, and it chastises our faith.

This disappointment often comes from us or others exercising our free will. It blows my mind that the God of the universe would choose to give us free will. Although He is sovereign,

He still does not force us to love Him, obey Him or be in relationship with Him. Knowing the character of God is vital to trusting Him and producing powerful, bold prayers. We can count on God not lying (Numbers 23:19) and not leaving us to go through all of this hard stuff alone (Deuteronomy 31:6).

Knowing the character of God is vital to trusting Him and producing powerful, bold prayers.

We can tell a lot about God by His names. Here are just a few from scripture that show us His character:

Jehovah Jireh, The LORD our Provider (Genesis 22:14)
Jehovah Rapha, The LORD our Healer (Exodus 15:26)
Jehovah Nissi, The LORD our Banner (Exodus 17:15)
Jehovah Shalom, The LORD our Peace (Judges 6:24)
Jehovah Raah, The LORD our Shepherd (Psalm 23:1)
Jehovah Tsidkenu, The LORD our Righteousness (Jeremiah 23:6)
Jehovah Shammah, The LORD is There (Ezekiel 48:35)

By coming to understand the true nature of God, we can begin to have bold prayers.

And these bold prayers matter. They keep us at the feet of Jesus. The more we are in conversation with Him, the less we are having circular conversations with ourselves! Thank God for that.

When we get so bold in our prayer life to trust Him with all of us, God is able to trust us with more of Him. That's exactly what happened to me in 2019 in Xai Xai, Africa. After those bold prayers my pastor prayed, we saw God move powerfully on our mission. We were ministering at our second of three conferences, had forty-nine women give their lives to Christ and eighteen women came to burn ceremonial cloths. One particular woman had been practicing ancestral worship for forty years. She threw everything into the fire and worshiped the one true and living God as they burned.

The more we are in conversation with God, the less we are having circular conversations with ourselves!

I asked her how we could pray for her. Our translator began to share with me that he's never seen her stand up straight. She had been bent over for years, and the pain would be so excruciating that she could only take a few steps at a time before she would stop in agony. Our team of women laid hands on her and prayed. We prayed boldly, with authority and belief for our God to move. As the team quieted, I asked her to test her back to see if the pain was gone. She began to straighten up and said that the pain was moving. I instructed the team to lay hands on her again as we continued to intercede for her healing. When we grew quiet, I told her to test it again. This time she said that the pain was moving down her leg. For a third time we laid hands on her, and this time before we finished, this woman who could not stand up straight began to jump. She was healed!

That day she left walking in an upright position, no longer bent. The next day was Sunday, and she came early before church to pray with our team. She was still standing tall. After our prayer time, all the women carried four chairs on their heads to take them from storage about a block away to the church. I thought I would be cool and cultural and put them on my head too. Just a few steps in, my neck was shaking, but not Veronica's. Veronica was walking out her healing, standing tall, praying and serving her God with her healing!

Fearful prayers sheepishly ask God for miracles and subconsciously expect nothing to happen. Fear does not hope, operate in authority or trust that God wants good things for us. It's time to be bold and pray prayers that you were once scared to pray. My fearless friend used to call these "bold, scary prayers."

Joshua's bold prayers and actions resulted in:

- ♥ Waters parting
- ♥ Walls falling down
- ♥ The sun standing still
- ♥ Conquests
- ♥ Prosperity
- ♥ His dreams coming to pass

Wherever you are on the fear factor, know that in the presence of God, you can be bold no matter what you feel! You are not some small, weak, purposeless and powerless woman. You are made perfect in love. Satan has no power over you. No weapon formed against you will prosper. God has delivered you from evil. Declare over your life today "Fear, you must go!" *Be bold.*

You can be bold no matter how you feel.

My Reflections

"Biblical obedience and submission is instant, holy, joyful, whole, and unconditional."

-Fred Markert

Walk in obedience to all that the Lord your God has commanded you, so that you may live and prosper and prolong your days in the land that you will possess.

Deuteronomy 5:33 (NIV)

Chapter 9
Be Obedient

We were a happy family of four and that was intentional. We are a ministry family, which means among many other amazing, miraculous things, we could also expect late nights, the need to be on call for whatever crisis or event would undoubtedly occur and unexpected guests, ringing the doorbell anytime throughout the week. We were not complaining, just acknowledging the demands that were forever reminding us that we could only handle so much. Plus we had a girl and a boy, so what more could we ask for?

Knowing that we were "done," I savored every precious moment with my son. One night, I was rocking my sweet baby boy to sleep when I heard the Holy Spirit whisper to me, "Why would you make that kind of decision without talking to me first?" It had been over a year since we had made the decision to not have any more kids, yet as soon as I heard these words, I knew exactly what decision the Lord was speaking about. I was embarrassed that we are ministers, but we never once asked God for His opinion on the matter.

Have you ever made a decision for God without first going to God? Did you make the decision because you were afraid of what God would say or because, like me, you were just limited by your logical way of thinking? At times, I feel we can make decisions without God's involvement because we want to be comfortable, in control and calculated in our plans to get our intended outcomes. Yet, as Christians we are to lay down our lives, our plans and our thinking so that we can walk the road that Christ has paved for us. It's less traveled, it has more twists and turns, but it is filled with the supernatural. If you are doing life or ministry in your own strength, I can guarantee you there's not much power in what you're accomplishing. If there's one thing I've learned over the years it's I'd rather have God's super over my natural any day of the week!

I'd rather have God's super over my natural any day of the week!

That night I sat in that rocking chair undone. I responded, "Lord, I'm so sorry for not coming to you with this. If it's your will for us to have another child, I need you to speak to Daniel and change his heart. I won't say anything to him about this conversation until he brings it to me, and then, I will know what your will is for us." I wanted Daniel to have his own experience with the Lord and for it to be something that we could share together, not something I was trying to convince him of.

The next week my husband flew out to launch our church campus in Mozambique. While he was gone, I had three people share with me that they really believed we were supposed to have another child. Still, I prayed, "Lord, thank you for the confirmations, but that's not what I asked for. I need you to change Daniel's heart." I kept praying for him during our time apart as I held close to me the Lord's words.

After being gone for two weeks, Daniel flew home, and the kids and I picked him up from the airport, and we went straight to eat so we could hear all about his trip. We sat there at the restaurant, soaking up all the stories. Then Daniel looks at me and says, "I think I want another one." I looked at the mozzarella cheese sticks and said, "There's plenty. Have another." He replied, "No, I want another one of those," as he pointed to my son, who was sitting in the highchair. My jaw dropped as he continued to go on and share with me that the whole time that he was gone he just kept hearing, "We are not complete. Three would make us complete." I started to cry and began to reveal to him all that had transpired over the last few weeks.

A year later, a blessing we never knew we needed came into the world. Not even in my wildest dreams could I have imagined our daughter, Kya Victoria, as beautiful and wonderful as she was. She was born full of vocal confidence, determination and wit. She was strong from day one; she even rolled over while we were still in the hospital! Nothing was going to keep her down or tell her what she could or couldn't do. I knew this girl was so special and she is. I cried just about every night when I would put her down to sleep, thinking, "I almost missed this!" I'm so thankful for a God who interrupts our plans, challenges our thinking and gives us what we would have missed if we had kept on our stubborn path.

The Ruin

I would characterize Joshua as a person who lived an obedient, faith-filled, prayerful life. He wasn't afraid to stand up to a crowd or step into the miraculous, even if it meant being an outcast. He took everything to the Lord, and God would speak so clearly to him about all of life's issues. That's why when I read Joshua chapter seven, I was a little taken back. In the chapter before, he had just royally defeated Jericho by simply walking around the wall seven times. Doesn't God have a way of humbling us? He doesn't use our skill to defeat the enemy;

God doesn't use our skill to defeat the enemy; He uses our obedience.

He uses our obedience. Now, they were facing the small city of Ai, which in Hebrew ironically means "The Ruin."

Joshua did not consult the Lord about a battle strategy; he instead sent a few spies, listened to their advice and executed it (Joshua 7:3-4). Have you ever used the phrase, "It's better to ask for forgiveness than to ask for permission"? Then you know how this is about to go down. Joshua sent out just three thousand men, which was a small fraction of his army, and with a very loose plan, they confidently walked up to Ai only to quickly turn around running with their tails between their legs all the way back to Joshua. Thirty-six men lost their lives that day and fear once again crushed the community (Joshua 7:5).

God's desire for us is to have utter reliance on Him through a relationship that is give and take, ask and obey. Now, I'm not one that goes to the grocery store and stands in the aisle praying over what cereal boxes to choose: "Lord, is it Cheerios or Lucky Charms?"—although after looking at the sugar content, maybe I should. However, as a practice, we should bring all of our decisions, great and small, to the Lord, asking him for His opinion on the matter, allowing the Holy Spirit to guide us and surrendering our path for His.

Joshua knew something was wrong, but he didn't know what it was, so he began asking God the "why" questions as he was weighing his losses. He didn't just lose men that day, he was also losing the confidence of the people, which really could have stirred up some old fears. Look how the Lord responded to him:

> *Stand up! What are you doing down on your face? Israel has sinned. . . . Joshua 7: 10-11 (NIV)*

There it is plain and simple! God knows more than we do, so that's why we go to Him first. He can save us so much heartache when we just communicate. In Matthew 6:11, we are encouraged to pray that the Lord would give us daily bread. I don't know about you, but I love to eat. In fact, when I don't eat, I get hangry and make poor choices. That's why I need to eat daily; in fact, my doctor tells me it's better for me to eat small meals throughout the day. The same is true in our spiritual life: we need daily bread, daily communion with God, to have wisdom and right thinking for whatever we face. We can't rely on yesterday's revelations to get us where we need to be today.

Yesterday's revelations won't divulge today's destination.

Unfortunately, we can get so busy we skip meals, and before we know it, we sacrifice good decision-making for Whataburger. Skipping our daily communion with God has more disastrous consequences than eating at Whataburger. Here's a thought to let linger: we can have as much of God as we want. Our measure of relationship with Him is up to our investment in the relationship. God is our helper and is always available to us, any time of the day and night. He's always there, and we are never a burden to Him. He wants to spend time with us daily, hourly, bringing us revelation and strategy ceasing unnecessary pain.

Ai almost ruined Joshua, and it wasn't because of his lack of skill (he had won many battles before) rather it was from a lack of obedience. Initially, a lack of obedience to put God first in his decision-making and then a lack of obedience he was completely unaware of. "Israel has sinned." I'm sure those words punctured Joshua's heart as he came to the knowledge that it wasn't the Lord who had brought bad fate on Israel but Israel's own foolishness that cost them lives that day. It's possible for us to be disobedient to God without even being aware of it.

Marion Jones represented America in the famous 2000 Olympics where she took home three gold and two bronze medals. Her glory was short-lived, as it was discovered that she had taken steroids. From her perspective, she was taking "supplements" that her trainer gave her. Little did she know that he had given her performance-enhancing drugs.[13] Isn't that just like the enemy to make us feel like we are taking one thing while all along he's seeking to manipulate us into engaging with things that will destroy us? It's in these discoveries that we wish we had been more alert to the details of our lives instead of "going with the flow." If Marion had just asked more questions or wanted to be more involved in every part of her training, it's possible she would not have found herself in this predicament. I'm sure many of us parents have felt this way at times when we've let things slide or just been "too tired" to investigate the little things that later turned into devastating things.

I once heard Marion say in an interview, "What was so hard was that I knew that I could have won without any of those drugs, and now I'll never have the chance to prove that." Hindsight is a brutal teacher. I don't want to live a life thinking of what I missed out on, how I could have been a better mother, where I should have utilized my time to make a greater impact or to have known God more. I want to make decisions that at the end of my life allow me to finish strong. It's not that we won't make mistakes, that's inevitable, but we can make conscious, informed, spirit-led decisions that positively impact our future. Marion disobeyed the rules, whether knowingly or unknowingly, and it cost her prison time, her medals, her career and her family. The decisions we make never just affect us, they have a domino effect on all of those around us.

Clarity

Maybe things are unclear, which can make it truly difficult to make the necessary changes. Clarity is key to our success. How many things can be lost through a lack of clarity? I'm sure you've experienced frustration from a lack of clarity. When I leave a meeting, I want to know who is supposed to do what by when. There is nothing that gets my blood boiling more than people who don't meet expectations or people who don't give expectations, and then expect you to read their minds! Are you with me? There isn't a limit to the chaos a lack of clarity creates.

But the Lord can help you work through the confusion to find clarity in what it is you need to change. God does not author confusion! The Lord wasn't going to leave Joshua hanging in the balance, left to his own thoughts to conjure up why he was walking through this defeat or blaming God for what felt like an "I'm turning my back on you" moment. No, he basically said, in the Celeste version of this story, "Put your big boy pants on. There's more to this story than what you know, and I'm about to show you what's been going on behind your back."

Often we want to look up and blame God when something goes wrong. We blame Him for not caring, or we wonder why He didn't intervene because He has the power to do anything, but we forget two things that are at play in all of this: free will and a fallen world. Let's focus for a bit on the first of these. Trust me, if I were God, free will would not be an issue, because you would all be doing things my way and with a smile on your face (back to that control thing again!), but thank God I'm not god for all of our sakes. Free will enables true relationships to be developed between an infinite God and finite humans. He gave us the gift to choose, and in that choice lies our worship. You see, to obey God is to worship God, to disobey God is to worship Satan. Seems harsh, a little too black and white, but it's true. It's clear.

Joshua, like many of us, was just going about living his life riding the high from his last victory oblivious to the sin that had crept in. We can all fall victim to this, and it feels like a tornado coming out of nowhere wreaking havoc on your home. I'm thankful God isn't afraid of twisters! Joshua might have been asking God the wrong questions, but God is not concerned with that; in fact, He invites our questions. If you are turning to God in your unwelcome storm, you're turning the right way regardless of the wrong understanding you might have. By turning to God, you give him permission to bring clarity to confusion.

If you are turning to God in your unwelcome storm, you're turning the right way regardless of the wrong understanding you might have.

It wasn't that Joshua didn't want to be obedient, he just didn't know what was going on in his own community, in his own home, so to speak. God makes it plain for him as He uncovers what had been hidden. When I'm going through a struggle and I just can't put my finger on it, I pray, "God, make it plain!" Have you ever known there was something not right, but you didn't know what it was? God is likely trying to get your attention, and the Holy Spirit is at work to guide you away from trouble, pointing out what the enemy is trying to hide and helping you to see what others are ignoring.

The Lord tells Joshua that there's sin in the camp, and then he gives him a strategy to locate it and destroy it. I love a good strategy meeting. This is one of my favorite things to do: sit around a table with brilliant minds and strategize on how to get the desired outcome. However, with the Lord, it doesn't quite work that way. He often delivers our next step, and then we try to negotiate it because our plan is easier, better and more peaceable . . . sound familiar? Or he gives us our next step, and we are partially obedient in hopes that some effort will get us a participation award, but that's just not how kingdom strategy works.

We have to be all in with God, and when we are, we will see God's hand move. Don't be afraid of that conversation the Lord's been telling you to have. Don't be afraid to go into your teen's room and look in places where you are scared of what you might find. Don't be afraid to ask that question or address that issue that's the elephant in the room. Don't be afraid to step out and/or to stand up! God will uncover what the enemy wants to hide, and he will show up so you will not have to do it alone. It's just who He is.

Joshua was likely shocked by the news that there was hidden sin, but even more mortified that someone in his camp had broken their covenant with God by taking things for themselves that belonged to God. Joshua clearly told the army to not touch these devoted items when they went into Jericho and that if they did, they would be a liability to Israel:

But keep away from the devoted things, so that you will not bring about your own destruction by taking any of them. Otherwise you will make the camp of Israel liable to destruction and bring trouble on it. All the silver and gold and the articles of bronze and iron are sacred to the Lord and must go into his treasury. Joshua 6:18-19 (NIV)

Everyone got the same memo! It's like the annoying kid in gym class that was late so everyone had to run an extra lap. After following God's investigation strategy, Joshua discovers that Achan, from the tribe of Judah, had taken many items from Jericho and buried them in his tent. I think he had an HGTV coveting experience. I guess he was planning for his new house that he was going to build in the Promised Land once they had finished all of their conquests. You're either a rule follower or someone who thinks rules are more like guidelines. I can be the latter depending on the situation, but that type of thinking has often been my own demise.

So Achan is obviously guilty as charged, but I'm wondering how in the world people did not see Achan take two hundred shekels of silver (that's over five pounds), a bar of gold weighing fifty shekels and a robe from the loot? Everyone in Israel knew the covenant they had made with the Lord and all that Joshua said, but they didn't care enough to call him out? His tent neighbor had to be suspicious of the shovel action that was happening next door! Can we please be a community that says something and doesn't turn a blind eye when we know that someone is about to walk into destruction?

Many years ago my husband and I were at a function when a well-meaning couple from our church came up to us. They began to share how the Lord was using us and, in particular, the ministry that had been flowing through me. They probably should have stopped there. While I believe their intentions were pure, I also have known gossip to be welcomed at their table, and out of their mouths started flowing how they had been so worried about me for such a long time during the trials that Daniel and I had to endure (none of which we had shared with them). They said that they didn't think I was going to get through it all but were amazed at how I came through them stronger and more powerful than before the hardships. We got in the car that night and my husband said, "Wasn't that awesome?" I responded, "No... In all the pain we walked through and felt so lonely in, not one time did they call us. They were so worried about us, but they couldn't pick up the phone?"

I wonder how many people we could save from destruction if we stopped talking about them and started to call them. Call them out. Call them up. Call them to encourage them. Send unexpected flowers. Deliver a thoughtful text. Invite them to lunch, not to try to get information to share with other onlookers, but just be a shoulder to cry on and a safe place of escape from all the noise. I think you would be surprised at how the little things mean so much to people when they are in pain. I can attest to the fact that a hug can truly heal. Be that kind of person. Be that kind of friend!

Do you know that a crushed ant emits an alarm pheromone that sends nearby ants into an attack frenzy and attracts more ants from farther away? That's a pretty cool superpower. When we see each other crushed, we should go on attack.

That doesn't mean male-bashing. That doesn't mean keying your boss's car. That doesn't mean praying that the house from the Wizard of Oz falls on someone. It doesn't mean we split the office and create an us-versus-them catastrophe. It means when we see a crushing spirit come over our friend, we say, "Oh no, sister, you are getting out of bed and leaving your house today!" We speak life where there is a stench of death. We call each other out instead of seeing destruction and allowing a passive spirit to keep us from speaking up. We pick each other up when we are down. We encourage each other. We help one another. We are obedient to the prompts of the Holy Spirit to see each other in our times of need.

We are only as accountable as we are honest.

When we are crushed, we don't need to put on a face that says "I'm perfectly fine" and keep going through our daily motions, because when we do, we keep the same route open for other "ants" to go down the same path. We need to emit an odor that says I need help. Accountability partners and mentors are such a huge thing right now. Everyone wants one, but we are only as accountable as we are honest. Stop trying to look perfect. You're not only hurting yourself but others that are watching you and your example to them.

Our strongest defense is community and transparency within that community. Our strongest offense is our testimonies. Our biggest platforms are the way we live our lives.

Our strongest defense is community and transparency within that community. Our strongest offense is our testimonies. Our biggest platforms are the way we live our lives. When we overcome, we can help others overcome. We can recognize the signs, smells and symptoms of their crushing. You can be honest with the temptations you are facing so you can have the help you need to overcome them. You can expose what you've been through so you can help others get through. You can help people understand that their struggle does not make them less than but can, in fact, be a turning point for them. We don't have to ache like Achan.

The truth be told, we've all been Achan or been affected by one. Disobedience can cost us everything, and everything was what it cost Achan. He and his family were stoned, burned and buried for what he hid out of disobedience. What's buried in your life that you need to burn before it burns you? Get it out! When we come into relationship with Jesus, the Holy Spirit will guide us and speak to us about things that need to be removed from our lives and things that we don't need to touch anymore. This is called the process of sanctification. When we choose Christ as our Lord and Savior, I wish it were like waving a magic wand and Abra Cadabra we are holy. But it is not that simple.

For me, I had all kinds of baggage by the time I truly surrendered my life to Christ, and I would find myself going to the same old things but having different feelings. I'd go to the club but didn't like how it made me feel anymore and realized I didn't need to go there anymore. I'd drop curse words in my conversations and think, "I don't like how that sounded or how I felt saying that." It was like I was wearing clothes that didn't fit anymore. I just kept shedding things over time that the

Holy Spirit would prompt me to release. Sometimes it felt great, and other times, it was a sacrifice. I've needed to remove relationships, TV shows, music, attitudes, offenses, bad habits like getting drunk, smoking, cursing and too many things to list, but they

Don't value what devalues you!

could have all burned me and buried me if I had not listened to the voice of God and been willing to expose all the things I once valued that devalued me.

Many years ago, I had a friend that had been through hell! One particular night she was really struggling, so I showed up on her doorstep with some flowers and a hug. She cried and said, "You do this? You just show up on people's doorsteps?" as tears flowed down her cheeks. God led me there that day. I was just being obedient, listening and leaning in. I asked her what she was doing, and she said, "I was closet smoking." I told her, "There's nothing you need to hide from me." She doesn't smoke anymore, but I'm even prouder that we have the kind of friendship where we don't have to hide stuff. We keep each other holy, set apart, for the greatness that God has called us to.

I don't know what Achan was going through that led him to the decision he made, but what I know is that when we go through stuff, God wants us to run to Him. Running to anything else will just bring a cancer-like problem to us. You can run to the refrigerator, the gym, video games, alcohol, shopping, sex, relationships or like Achan, stealing, but it will just be another disappointment for you. Instead, be obedient and run to Jesus.

Come to me, all you who are weary
and burdened, and I will give you rest.
Matthew 11:28 (NIV)

Come to Jesus with it all. Maybe the Lord has been telling you some things through this chapter, and/or maybe He's affirming some things that you need to do but it will cost you. I want to encourage you with this: obedience will cost you, but disobedience will cost you more. Bring it all to Jesus and allow the Holy Spirit to empower and embolden you to obey. Whatever you think is too big or too hard, it's not. Don't bury your potential. *Be obedient* no matter what.

> *Obedience will cost you, but disobedience will cost you more.*

My Reflections

"It's not all about talent. It's about dependability, consistency, and being able to improve. If you work hard and you're coachable, and you understand what you need to do, you can improve."

-Bill Belichick

Give instruction to a wise man, and he will be still wiser; teach a righteous man, and he will increase in learning.

Proverbs 9:9 (ESV)

Chapter 10
Be Coachable

Learning to drive requires a dependence on your instructor, a coachable mindset and a willingness to adjust and shift with the road's demands. The unfortunate truth is that no matter how great of a driver you are, you will undoubtedly experience unexpected collisions that will cost you, but my encouragement to you today is to also allow these unwanted crashes to coach you instead of crush you.

Allow unwanted crashes to coach you instead of crush you.

At fifteen, I came home from school upset and frustrated. In an effort to comfort me, my mom said, "Let's go for a drive." I got in the car, and as I was backing out, I heard the most awful noise; it was metal colliding with concrete. The steps on the side of our house hit the exhaust pipe as I backed up unaware of its proximity. The exhaust pipe completely bent in half, rendering it useless. Tears filled my eyes and adrenaline ran through my body, causing my heart to race and my hands to shake. Thoughts of my dad exploding in anger immediately filled my mind. I cautiously looked out the window with dread as my eyes locked with my dad, who had witnessed the whole incident. To my surprise, he was not exploding with anger, he was exploding with laughter. That night he came into my room with a chunk of that metal exhaust pipe that he had sawed off as a token from the day's adventure. He did not judge me, he embraced me and coached me for my next drive.

Similarly, we can view ourselves like I viewed that exhaust pipe: broken, bent, dirty, worthless and unforgivable. In addition, we see our Father God as mean-spirited, ready to judge us and condemn us, but those were never God's thoughts toward us. God is not waiting for us to mess up or boastfully celebrating our losses. Instead, His arms are open wide as He desires us to see what He sees: value and worth. He extends His hands to us to help us up and coaches us to greatness.

A good coach invests time into those with a teachable spirit. I've never been athletic in my life and still have nightmares about being the last one picked for every game in gym class, but the one thing I always want said of me is that I'm coachable. I want to grow. I want to learn. I want to be better. I want to improve the teams I now get to play on!

Stand Up

When the Lord told Joshua to stand up, He didn't want to hear about Joshua's losses at Ai. He already knew it all. He coached Joshua to get up and pay attention to what was really going on to cause all of the damage to begin with. Sometimes we've got to stop crying long enough to realize that we might be the source of all of the frustration that led to the tears. It's easy in hardship to ask why questions, blame the people around you and even take offense when well-meaning people are just trying to help you.

> *'We've got to stop crying long enough to realize that we might be the source of frustration that led to all of the tears.*

As a pastor, I have had people upset with me because I called them to see how they were when I learned they were sick, but in the same week had a different person upset because I didn't call them in their time of sickness. At times, it can feel impossible to please everyone, and we all handle pain differently. When you feel defeated, disappointed or your heart aches, do the most courageous thing you can: really take a deeper look at your own life and heart and remain coachable.

I was once callously handed a piece of paper, by a leader, that listed every poor quality of my leadership that had been shared with them. I was told that I should take those words with me into my future roles. I went home, and as I looked over the words that were written, they pierced me. Admittedly, because I was going through a personally painful season, I had put every relational gift I had on the back-burner, unconsciously distrusting people and building walls that made me unapproachable. Instead of being myself, I tried to earn my worth through works, which resulted in burnout for me and the team around me. Approval by production left me emptier than ever.

Tears rolled down my cheeks as the feelings of rejection deepened with every word written. I don't even remember those words now, but I owned them—all of them. At the time, I felt like no one was rooting for me or willing to coach me to be better, but I knew the Lord could show me how to grow through this if I stood up and took responsibility. In hindsight, I realize that most people are not intentionally trying to harm you, they are just not aware of or sensitive to your pain. We can't expect the world to rally around and adjust their communication and expectations based on our complex history or unshared hurts. In addition, not everyone in authority is meant to steward your heart. They are stewarding a vision. Although hard conversations can be hurtful, they are also an invitation to go deeper in our healing and to go further in our calling.

The enemy's intention was to label me and have me carry those words for the rest of my life, but that's not who I was, and more importantly, I had a deep conviction that the Lord was not done with me yet. Maybe that's a power statement for you today: *God's not done with you yet!* You can take responsibility without taking criticism as your identity. No matter what was said to you or about you, that's not who you are. You may have some work to do, but that's not your identity!

Honor

There's a hard choice you're going to have to make when you go through times that challenge your character. You can respond by your flesh (emotions) or by your spirit, which grows you. You can't have it both ways, and trust me, if you choose the latter, the emotions don't go away and it will not be easy, but it will enlarge you and your impact.

Personally, I want impact more than reactive emotions that often leave me feeling even more shameful and alone. I want people to be amazed that no matter what comes my way, I grow. There are only two times throughout the scriptures that it records Jesus being amazed. The first was because of belief (Luke 7:9) and the second was because of unbelief:

Jesus left there and went to his hometown, accompanied by his disciples. When the Sabbath came, he began to teach in the synagogue, and many who heard him were amazed.

"Where did this man get these things?" they asked. "What's this wisdom that has been given him? What are these remarkable miracles he is performing? Isn't this the carpenter? Isn't this Mary's son and the brother of James, Joseph, Judas and Simon? Aren't his sisters here with us?" And they took offense at him.

*Jesus said to them, "A prophet is not without **honor** except in his own town, among his relatives and in his own home." He could not do any miracles there, except lay his hands on a few sick people and heal them. **He was amazed at their lack of faith.** Mark 6:2-6 (NIV)*

Where honor is absent, a lack of faith is revealed and/or produced. Honor says more about who we are than about

Honor says more about who we are than about what's been done to us.

what's been done to us. You can look at a situation and feel justified in your flesh because of the narrative surrounding it, or you can choose the high road and do the hard things. I've always wanted to live a miraculous life, and miracles simply cannot follow someone who can only honor when everything is going well. Honor is counterintuitive to our emotions. Our emotions want to build a case against people to support our offense, and as a result, it seeds a root of bitterness.

Honor is counterintuitive to our emotions.

But when we choose to be obedient through honor, God will prosper us even in times of affliction. My prayer in seasons of suffering is that the fruit of my life will show the deeper places of my heart. I want Jesus to know my willingness to be changed and moved by Him, no matter how I was handled or mishandled. As a youth, I was super rebellious, especially if I felt attacked in any way; it was a defense mechanism. As an adult, I can easily revert back to those ways, but instead of submitting to an old way of doing things, I harness those emotions to become useful. I have determined to be rebellious against my own flesh and remain coachable to become who God wants me to be. He will strengthen my character as I allow Him to shape me. When I want to respond with anger from hurt, I instead try to acknowledge the emotion with humility and determine to be resilient to make necessary changes. I will become better, not bitter.

Truly believing in who God is will strengthen our resolve to rise up to our full potential. His Word anchors our futures and sets our hopes on His character—as we build our own. We can be secure in these truths no matter how grim our situation may be:

- ♥ He has a plan for me (Jeremiah 29:11).
- ♥ He is good (Nahum 1:7).
- ♥ He will prosper me (Romans 8:28).
- ♥ He will fight for me (Exodus 14:14).
- ♥ He won't leave me (Deuteronomy 31:6).
- ♥ He will give me direction (Proverbs 3:5-6).

In this particular season of refinement, I began to go to work by facing the fact that my problems were more a reflection of my own life than others'. I had many bad hurts and habits that hindered my leadership, and by acknowledging that, in a healthy way, I could also know that just because I had messed up didn't mean that I was a mess-up. Those things written on that paper were not a reflection of my heart, so I had to labor to ensure that what I do truly reflects who I am.

Labor to ensure that what you do truly reflects who you are.

Cycle of Change

Even in times where accusations are so outlandish, there will usually be a sliver of truth if we are being honest. The devil is known as the father of lies, but what makes him so good at it is that he uses the tiniest piece of truth to make you question yourself and God. The same sliver of truth can make you paranoid of other people. If we can cut through the lies, get to that truth and devote ourselves to development, the truth will truly set us free.

Listening to a leadership podcast one day helped me to do just that. I learned about a cycle of change that really awakened me to the "how to" in the process that seemed to be taking longer than I would have hoped. I want to share this with you now in hopes that you too can make strides to accurately reflect who you are even when you are under pressure, out of place, or walking through difficulty.

Cycle of Change[14]

Unconscious Incompetence: Not knowing there is an issue, but causing damage because there is one.

Conscious Incompetence: Being able to recognize there is an issue, but not being able to change the behavior yet.

Conscious Competence: Consciously making an effort to change behavior, but it does not feel natural.

Competence: Implementing a behavior for an extended period of time to where now it is a natural habit.

Let me give you some insight into how this works. When I was learning how to drive, my mom took me out to an empty football stadium. The first time is probably awkward for any new driver, but especially for me. I kept trying to use my left foot. My left foot was on the brake and my right foot was on the gas, so imagine the whiplash my mom was experiencing! In our listed categories above, we would call this stage of my driving game "Unconscious Incompetence." I'd never driven before so I had no idea what I was doing was wrong, but that doesn't mean it was any less wrong, it just means that I was oblivious to the wrongdoing.

After a few minutes of driving like this, my mom realized what I was doing and said, "Celeste, you are going to kill us! Don't use your left foot to drive, keep it off to the side, and use your right foot to go between the gas and the brake." OK, so now I knew the issue, but that didn't mean that I could fix it right away. The next time we went driving I kept catching my left foot sneaking over, and I just felt like a total dud. I was now in the "Consciously Incompetent" category.

Now, this is a step in the right direction, but it doesn't feel great. It actually feels demoralizing! At this stage you just think you're never going to get it right, but that's wrong thinking. You've probably been in this bad behavior for quite a long time, so it's going to take some time to work you out of it. The fact that you can now recognize when you are doing it is a sign that you are almost ready to go to the next step.

The next time I went driving, I consciously (in my head) would say to my left foot, "Foot, stay still." Did this feel weird? Umm, ya! But it worked, and even though it wasn't a habit for me, the conscious decision I was making led to new healthy patterns for my driving life. This stage is called "Conscious Competence."

Now we get to go to my favorite part of this illustration, "Competence." I have been driving for decades now, and I drive so often that sometimes I get to a location and I really don't remember the drive there! It's like muscle memory for me. I don't have to think of feet, blinkers or any other navigation instrument. I just start the car and go. I'm a competent driver. End of story. (Thank you, mom, for your patience.)

This is what it can look like in a work setting: imagine you're in a large meeting, and afterward someone from the team says to you, "Hey, you kept interrupting people in there. It felt like you didn't care about what anyone else had to say." Now, in your mind, you were just so excited to share your idea that you were completely oblivious to the fact that you were making the team feel devalued. You were consciously incompetent, but now that you know, you can begin your process of change.

The next meeting you're in, you have an idea that pops into your head, and you just start blurting out your ideas, but halfway through your thought, you see the looks on the faces of those at the table as you realize you just cut a team member off. You begin to rehearse the conversation your very brave coworker shared with you. Red-faced you finish up and kick yourself for not being able to control your tongue, but hey, you recognized when you did it, you were consciously incompetent, and that's something to celebrate. When you can be self-aware enough to acknowledge your shortcomings and conscious enough to begin to recognize them when they come up, you are doing better than most people. Note that being self-aware does not mean you have to be self-conscious. This step takes a lot of humility and commitment.

Now you have another opportunity to be a great functioning, contributing part of a real team that values each other. So now when you are sitting there in that boardroom and the lightbulb goes off in your head, you take out a pen and jot it down because someone else is talking, and you're not going to interrupt them. You are determined not to. You are literally in your head saying, "Wait your turn" over and over. They stop talking, you compliment their thoughts and then you begin to share your own with the team. You leave the table that day with a win! It may have not felt natural, but you were choosing to be consciously competent.

Many meetings later, you and the team are just flowing with each other, encouraging one another to debate and inspire without railroading, domineering or shutting down creative flow. You did that! Imagine, you can do that. Whatever it might be for you, take the time to choose to change your behaviors that have the opportunity to reflect the best of what's in you and bring out the best of the team around you.

Positive Impact

Years later, a girl joined my team. I felt for her because I knew she had struggled with the perceptions of others that she had built for herself through some bad habits. At our first meeting,

I gave her a piece of paper and asked her to begin an exercise. In the first column I asked her to write down how she felt people in her work space viewed her. When she was done, she read them to me, with many tears running down her tender cheeks. I asked her, "Do these words you wrote reflect your heart?" to which she answered, "No."

Next, I had her write down who she is as a person, and she read them to me. Her list was just as long as all the negative chatter that had filled her paper on column one. I said, "OK, so can I coach you to begin to change your behaviors to reflect who you truly are?" After she said a grateful, humble, willing yes, I watched this beautiful young woman become one of the most valuable players on the team. Before she left my office that day, I had her tear up that paper. I didn't want her carrying any negative words into her new role. I wanted her to carry the confidence of the call to which she was being called.

Each week she chose to do the hard things. She was coachable by asking for feedback, taking correction and, ultimately, relearning how to communicate in a way that brought an incredible lift and discerning voice to the team. I often see women who have strong tendencies excuse themselves from being molded. From one strong woman to another, allow the refining of the Lord to give a furnace for your fire. A fire unbridled will burn everyone, but if you steward it in the right way, the same fire can be a fierce furnace to warm, protect and illuminate the darkness. I love to watch a misunderstood woman put form around the substantive gifts God has placed in her. There is purpose in your strength so use it wisely.

Just as our decisions can affect others for the negative, how we choose to respond when we are aware of our mistakes and shortcomings can positively impact others. By acknowledging the pain you have caused someone and working to make changes moving forward, you show them that they matter. Don't beat yourself up! You get to decide who you will be, and when others fail, you can have the same grace and choose to build them up not tear them down. We can do the hard work to bring the best out of ourselves, and through the help of the Holy Spirit, He can shape those rough edges around us and heal all that has wounded us on the inside so we can prosper.

Or . . . we can simply settle for "This is just who I am, and I can't change." What are you going to do? Who are you going to become? How are you going to handle being mishandled by others? Will you grow or will you go? It would have been easy for me to walk away the day I was handed that piece of paper, but I don't have a job, I have a calling! A calling isn't easy, but you can't run away from it or it will haunt you. So, are you going to stand up and get to work, or are you going to quit? I am far from perfect, but I'm not where I used to be. I have determined in my heart to stand, to posture myself to move forward toward the promises of God by staying coachable.

I press on toward the goal to win the prize for which God has called me heavenward in Christ Jesus.
Philippians 3:14 (NIV)

Many years later, the same person that handed me that sheet of paper worked with me on a project. To be honest, I had some unresolved offense at the way I was, in my eyes, mishandled instead of coached. After the completion of the project we collaborated on, we visited at my request. I didn't want to make assumptions about how I was viewed, keeping me fearful and my gifts restrained, so I asked the hard questions and exposed my heart and hurt.

To my amazement, that same person communicated to me that seeing me lead was one of the best parts of the project. What the enemy meant to use to harm me, God used to grow me. He humbled me, and He was my helper and my coach as I allowed Him into my hurt, so He could heal my pain and reposition me for greatness.

The Lord shaped me, and my rough edges, into who He had always created me to be because I was faithful to be obedient to His voice and instruction, even in times that felt harsh and cruel. In return, with a gentle hand and guidance from the Holy Spirit, I have coached countless others who resembled who I used to be. Just like me, they have had so much raw potential but needed purpose to be drawn out of them.

The purposes of a person's heart are like deep water.
But one who has understanding brings them out.
Proverbs 20:5 (NIRV)

Mud or Clay

For a moment, I want you to think about yourself in two forms: mud or clay. You can quickly tell the difference between clay and mud by this: in the presence of the sun, the clay softens and mud hardens. What do you feel when confronted with areas of your life either by a person, preaching, teaching or even reading your Bible? When in the presence of Christ, is your heart soft? Are you moldable and pliable with the Potter's hands as your guide? When you hear something you don't like, do you immediately begin to build walls, or do you ask God to search your heart and help you to change? We all have work to do. None of us are perfect, but we are all valuable to the Potter.

> *This is the message that came to Jeremiah from the Lord: "Jeremiah, go down to the potter's house. I will give you my message there." So I went down to the potter's house and saw him working with clay at the wheel. He was making a pot from clay. But there was something wrong with the pot. So the potter used that clay to make another pot. With his hands he shaped the pot the way he wanted it to be.*
> *Jeremiah 18:1-4 (ERV)*

Have you ever felt like the pot, like there is something wrong with you? Some translations say "but the pot was marred," which translates in Hebrew as "ruined." I've felt a bit ruined in past seasons. Maybe your plans have been ruined before, you've experienced ruined relationships or you've messed up so bad you feel you've ruined everything! Here's the interesting part shared with us in the verse above: the Potter used that clay, the messed-up, marred, ruined clay to make another pot. If I were the Potter, I'd just throw away the clay because there's nothing wrong with the Potter! All the issues are wrapped up in the clay, yet the Potter still sees potential in the clay, purpose in the clay, value in the clay. Then He shapes the pot into the vessel He wants it to be.

Just like Ai meant ruined, it could have ruined Joshua. It could have ruined his reputation, his confidence and derailed him from completing his mission, but instead Joshua remained coachable. He turned to God in his mess, and as we learned, God gave him strategy to overcome sin and then He coached him to be strong and courageous as he faced his adversary once again. He was pliable in the Potter's hands.

I can imagine what we sometimes look like in the Potter's hand: stubborn and unwilling to yield. I bet we look ridiculous sometimes, like trying to put clothes on a two-year-old. They wiggle and squirm, and they have opinions that make little to no sense. I'm so thankful to have passed that stage with my kids; sorry if you are there right now, but I promise it gets better! However, then they grow into teenagers, and you will still be fighting over what they are wearing. Have you ever heard these words, "Everyone is wearing this," or "Mom, you just don't want me to have fun!" as if fun has anything to do with it at all!

We sometimes do the same thing: question God's intentions with us, especially in messed-up seasons of our lives. But consider the time and attention that the Potter has invested in the vessel, God's intentions are pure, and we are His focus. Time is our biggest resource, and the Potter's full being, all His energy, is tied up with what's on the wheel! His foot pumps the pedal on the floor to spin the wheel, and in order to keep everything steady, He keeps the top wheel so close to His core, which gives Him control. His hands are constantly shaping the clay as the wheel spins. It's tedious, meticulous and beautiful all at the same time. The Potter's design is to make something useful from the clay. He wants to make our situations useful. He wants to shape us in such a way we will be prepared for every season!

> *The Potter's design is to make something useful from the clay.*

However, it's tempting to get off the wheel too soon. We think we are ready to be used, but we haven't finished the process. We leave without a blessing. We launch something without prayer. We step into a relationship before we've dealt with the pain of the last one. Can I encourage you with something today? It takes a long time to make something beneficial. We've come into a microwave culture that values instant over consistent. How much time does it take for a baby to grow up to be able to help with the laundry? How long does it take to see fat turned into muscle? What about learning a new language and having a full conversation in that language? In the same way, why are we so impatient with ourselves and the development process that needs to occur for us to be fruitful?

Stay on the wheel! Keep showing up. Keep doing the hard things. Keep stewarding hope. Keep challenging your faith. Remain coachable. You never know when an opportunity will come your way, and at that time, God will show you, it's your moment to get off the wheel!

Get off the Wheel

One week I was sitting in our staff chapel and our pastor over our prison ministry was sharing a testimony about what was happening at one of our women's units. When he finished, our senior pastor looked at me and said, "We should be doing our women's conference in the prison." I glanced at our prison pastor and confidently said, "We'll get right on it." In a month's time, we hosted our very first event and have now seen thousands of inmates ministered to and hundreds of salvations and water baptisms! I had no idea that this opportunity was going to come to me, nor did I know how much I would love to minister behind bars, but it's truly been the highlight of my life. It was a get-off-the-wheel moment, and I didn't know if I was ready or what to expect, but the Potter showed me I was useful and all that was in my past would be a tool to me on this assignment.

In 2021, I went into the prison and spoke to the women on the "I am(s)" of life. I had the inmates write down critical words that people had said to them throughout their lives. Once they were done, they brought their paper to a prayer partner, and as they shared, we broke the word curses off of their lives. My pockets were full of torn-up words of hate, rejection, lies and filth that had infiltrated the hearts of these women. If you only knew those words written you would understand why they got where they were. One particular girl had been moved throughout the day. On her paper she took a very different approach and wrote who she now saw that she was in Christ, not what she had been labeled. She wrote:

"I am more than I think I am worth. I am not what people think about me. I am not ugly. I am not dumb. I am not a liar. I am not useless. I am not naive. I am not weak. I am not just my sins. I am not who I used to be."

This beautiful girl with dark braided hair got into the baptismal and wept. I asked her what baptism meant to her and she said: "I am not a monster. God loves me." Can I tell you, you're not who you think you are? You're not the things the enemy whispers to you at night. You're not your mistakes. You're not defined by your failure. You're a success in the making! You're a comeback girl! You're loved by the creator of the universe, and there is purpose and potential left in your clay. Get off the wheel when it is time to get to work, then get back on the wheel to continuously grow. God's not done with you yet!

Joshua got right back on the wheel after his defeat at Ai, and the Lord coached him with a plan and a promise of deliverance:

> *You shall do to Ai and its king as you did to Jericho and its king, except that you may carry off their plunder and livestock for yourselves. Set an ambush behind the city. Joshua 8:2 (NIV)*

This time Joshua didn't carelessly send his men into battle; instead, he was obedient to the Lord's every command:

> *Then the Lord said to Joshua, "Hold out toward Ai the javelin that is in your hand, for into your hand I will deliver the city." ... So Joshua held out toward the city the javelin that was in his hand.*

> *For Joshua did not draw back the hand that held out his javelin until he had destroyed all who lived in Ai. Joshua 8:18, 26 (NIV)*

Not only was he coachable, he was resilient and unbreakable in his form. When Moses held the rod above his head, he got tired, but when Joshua held out his javelin, he had such a strength in his vessel he did not falter! When we take the time to go through the coaching process, we invest in the strength of our vessel. For me, I want to be a strong vessel, useful for the purposes of God, even if that means more time on the wheel and work behind the scenes. I want to expose weak places that, if not properly molded, could break me. I don't want any platform my character cannot sustain, so my continued prayer is, God make me into what you want me to be!

About six months after I spoke to my new friend in the prison, in that baptism pool, I saw her again at another event. She met me at the door and greeted me with a smile from ear to ear. Her countenance was different from the last time I saw her. She said to me with joy and wit, "I keep trying to submit my letter of resignation to the state, but they just won't accept it!" Although she had once again been denied for parole since I had last seen her, she would go before the review board again in just a few months' time. She wanted to go home, but she said if she got denied she still had four more conferences left to look forward to before her sentence was up! She knew God still had more for her on the wheel. She still had something to look forward to as God molded her and shaped her and so do you.

Whether you're going through a season of coaching or you're standing on the other side of the hard work of change, be all in with Jesus. Just like me, you are not the sum total of your mistakes, yet know that there's beauty and purpose in your pain. God had always known who I was and who He had made me to be, but now I would get to see what God sees. Each subsequent year, I felt more and more alive in my calling and my impact expanded to lengths and depths I could never have imagined. All of this was achieved without striving or fear; it was birthed through pure obedience. No longer would I stay in shame and cycles that didn't align with God's purposes for me. I want to encourage you with this: you are who God says you are. *Be coachable* because God wants to lead you to victory!

"Life isn't about finding yourself.
It's about discovering who
God created you to be."

-Author Unknown

Your hands made me
and formed me; give me
understanding to learn your
commands. May those who fear
you rejoice when they see me, for I
have put my hope in your word.

Psalm 119:73-74 (NIV)

Chapter 11
Be You

Receiving a promotion in my mid-twenties, my supervisor, who was the majority owner of the company, sat me down to talk with me about expectations moving into my new role. He looked at me with sincerity and honesty and said, "You have two things working against you: you're female and you're pretty." I was a little stunned that he communicated such raw, unfiltered caution to me, and I read between the lines, just like he wanted me to. The men wouldn't respect me and the women would be jealous of me.

I knew I was in a "man's world." That was clear from the time a coworker was found watching porn at work and just got a little "talking to," which was good enough to cover the offense as they laughed behind closed doors. The mail clerk would often walk past women's desks and linger so he could look down our shirts as he dropped off files. It was a constant frustration. In addition, women weren't generally in higher positions in this line of work; men would get the business and women would do the paperwork. I was grateful to be a part of a firm that was changing the norm in that regard.

It took me many years and many mistakes to learn how to be a woman and earn respect and sometimes demand it. If you don't respect yourself, no one else will. When I was fifteen, I got my first job at an indoor snow cone shop, hoping to save up to buy my first car. I was excited and nervous my first day and the flutters weren't put to ease when in my first encounter with a coworker, who was a teenage boy, not much older than I was, told me, referring to the owner who was in his fifties, "Don't ever go into the back room alone with him." I was taken back by these words, but I also had a friend that got a job with me, and I didn't want to back out on her.

If you don't respect yourself, no one else will.

Each time I worked, I would learn more and more gossip about the owner and how he would buy young women breast implants and all sorts of things about the places he could be found at night. One day while I was at the counter pouring juice into a snow cone, the owner bent down to get another flavor of juice from underneath the counter, and on his way back up, he squeezed my leg and commented about how he had liked my body. That should have been enough to send me running home to talk to my parents, but to be honest, I just didn't know what to do with it. These were not things we talked about in my home, and this was my first experience in the workplace. I wanted to do a good job, and I thought I could handle it.

A few months went by, and up to this point, I had never been in the position to be alone at work with my boss, as there were always other employees and people around. On this particular day, someone no-showed, and we got slammed! After about an hour or so of fulfilling nonstop orders, the shop was empty. I sat on the counter, as we often did, to give my feet a break, and when I did, he came over to me, pinned me down with his hands on both sides of me, and began to tell me that he was so frustrated with the rest of the staff, but he could always count on me and that was why he loved me so much. I felt trapped and didn't know what to do. He then went in to kiss me. I quickly turned my head and leaned backward; unfortunately, he still was able to put his lips on my cheek. I felt violated.

I went home and held it all in. I just didn't know what to do. A few days later when it was time for me to go in for my next shift, I told my mom that I had planned on quitting that day. She started to tell me that in our house we don't quit jobs until we find another one and we give a proper notice. The pressure of everything I was holding inside erupted as I harshly interrupted her with the details of my experience. Her tone quickly changed, and she told me to quit that day. She waited for me in the car as I went in alone to confront my boss. It was a good lesson for me to stand up for myself and have hard conversations face to face. I stood right in front of him, fifteen years old, and bravely let him know that I wouldn't be coming back. He had the audacity to ask me why, and I told him, "You know what you did!" and I left.

Later that day my mom and dad paid him a visit. My dad had many valiant moments in my life, and this was certainly one of them. I do wish I had been a fly on the wall. My mom told me that he ripped the guy a new one and said, "The only reason I'm on this side of the counter and you're not on the floor is because I'm a pastor!" I've seen my dad mad and know for a fact he could have punched his lights out.

Every place I worked I experienced some type of unwelcome advance and had to learn how to work through it, how to stand up for myself and how to not cave to societal norms and pressures. I wish I had done many things differently, but over time, the Holy Spirit taught me how to walk in discernment, authority, purity and honor even when my environment was set against me. I learned through these experiences that if I don't know my worth,

If you don't know your worth, then others will cheapen it.

then others will cheapen it and exploit it, and I will lose who I am with every worthless exchange. Know who you are and be confident to be you.

Friendships that Shape You

The second part of what my boss had warned me of, that other women would be jealous of me, was hard to hear. Friendships had always meant so much to me, but I had also experienced the brutality of mean girls. Now that I was an adult with a professional job, I thought maybe we'd be over high school ways. However, according to him, I would have to work twice as hard to win over women relationally because of jealousy and judgements. I had a target on my head before I would get a chance to even have a conversation. It's so strange to grow up your whole life feeling like you are ugly, then hear your boss tell you that women would hate you and your success in your career could be jeopardized because you are "pretty."

Before we go any further, can I tell you something? *You are beautiful.* There's no reason why any woman should feel less than another woman because of how she looks or anything else for that matter. The world wants us to be pit against each another so we won't rally for worthy causes, and so we will spend ridiculous amounts of time and money to become what we already are in the sight of God: beautiful. Your body has given to you and supported you no matter how mean or cruel you've treated it, so learn to love the body God gave you! Take care of yourself to steward the gift of life, *and* be nice to you!

Now that I was told how others viewed me, I found myself walking into every room thinking, "She hates me. She hates me. She hates me." I felt like I was working out of a complete deficit. I never liked everyone's eyes being on me to start with, and now the thought of having to give a presentation or meet someone new gave me complete anxiety. It's an awful thing to constantly be reminded that people don't like you. Despite my advancement in the company, the underbelly of success was the perpetual fear that women were judging me before they even knew me.

Have you felt like that before? Judged. Have you ever thought, "If I were a man, this would be a non-issue for me!" My mom would always tell us girls growing up, "You can do anything a man can do," but was that really the case? It has seemed that the more I did or achieved, the more women hated me. A man's success gets him honor and respect from other men, while a woman's success marks her for instant rejection. Women tend to see each other as obstacles to success instead of an inspiration to become successful and teammates that cheer each other on. It's easier to look at someone's success and list the reasons why they got what they didn't deserve versus truly evaluating our own successes and failures and learning from them both. Do not let other women's evaluations of you dim your light and choose to be a woman who cheers other women on.

Women tend to see each other as obstacles to success instead of an inspiration to become successful.

I had two coworkers that handled the same situation very differently. One was male, and when he had been looked over for an opening that would seem like a natural promotion for him, he went to his supervisors and said, "If I'm not being considered for this promotion, I need to know why so I can grow." His boldness and also humility to confront his supervisor and face the fact that there may be areas of growth needed gave him an opportunity to lay out what he would do if he was in the role. At the end of the day, he got the job.

Then I saw a female in the same situation, and she had been there more than once, passed over for promotion. Instead of asking the hard questions and exposing her limitations, she became bitter and never went any further. She lost her joy, her drive, and her fingers pointed everywhere except for herself. She really didn't value herself enough to do the hard things, and unfortunately, that's where the enemy will have a field day with you. He'll help you insert your deepest darkest insecurities and lies he's fed you all your life as the reason why you are not where you want to be. When we fill in the reasons for other people, it's always a million times worse than if we would just face it head-on. Remember, God can do anything with a willing heart, so even if there are legitimate things keeping you from promotion, a humble spirit can take you to the next step.

Another common threat to women in our leadership is control. If we are not getting the desired result, we frequently use our influence to manipulate our outcome. Using the people around you to get where you want to go won't elevate you, it will disgrace you. Maybe you've experienced this too, but there have been too many times in my life where I have questioned myself

Using the people around you to get where you want to go won't elevate you, it will disgrace you.

because I lost a friend after I received a promotion or an opportunity or when they felt they weren't getting further advancement through the use of our friendship. The enemy uses these hurtful experiences to bring accusations against our person. It sounds like:

- ♥ You're not likable.
- ♥ You're too much.
- ♥ You're not enough.

- ♥ Leadership is lonely.
- ♥ If only you would have done [fill in the blank].

Controlling people will kill your confidence as they conspire to steal your influence. Like the enemy, they'll get into your world and say things that make you feel good, but at the opportune time, they will make a move to get what they want from you. If they don't succeed, you can say goodbye to your so-called friend. It's important to realize that what they did is not a reflection of who you are.

The older I get, the more I realize I don't need that many friends. Not everyone likes me, but that doesn't mean no one likes me. I'd rather have quality over quantity. I have a few amazing people in my inner circle who I can call day or night, show up unannounced and be completely unfiltered with. They have permission to challenge me, they are relentless prayer warriors on my behalf, they love my whole family and they do

Not everyone likes me, but that doesn't mean no one likes me.

not have to tiptoe around any area of my life. They don't want anything from me, except for me! That's what your inner circle should look like. If you don't have an inner circle, pray that God will show you who to trust. That's what I did so many years ago when I felt like I could never trust again. Let me tell you, you can trust again, and it's worth it to be able to just *be you* with people that love you.

Stay True to Yourself

If we aren't careful, we are not only hurt at the loss of what we thought was friendship, but we also will be manipulated by the enemy to hate ourselves and/or change ourselves for the sake of acceptance. The truth is God will expose the hearts of people, but in His time and in His way. Remember, it's God who brings promotion!

We can be the biggest barriers to our own success.

No one can stand in the way of where God wants us to go except for ourselves. We can be the biggest barriers to our own success. If you are seeing someone as an advancement barrier, you are looking in the wrong direction. Have you ever read about the life of Joseph in the Bible? God used every single roadblock to actually pave the way to success.

He was sold into slavery → put in charge of Potiphar's house →

Accused of sexual harassment → put in prison → promoted to second in command.

Seems so unlikely, right? God won't be mocked by wicked schemes to keep you from your destiny. He'll use everything to promote you where He wants you to be.

For promotion cometh neither from the east, nor from the west, nor from the south. But God is the judge: he putteth down one, and setteth up another.
Psalm 75:6-7 (KJV)

However, God also won't make us choose the right path when faced with unfair circumstances. The fact is we can't change human nature, our natural hunger to feed our earthly desires, but we can change our perspective and strengthen our resolve to be who God created us to be no matter what temptations and challenges we endure. What's so wonderful about Jesus is that He too had the same hurts and temptations, but He never allowed them to change who He was. It seemed as though the more Jesus was hurt, the deeper He loved. When I've been hurt, my instinct is to withdraw, to quit, to run away, to build a wall, but that's not who I am at the core. I'm not a quitter. I've never been a runner in any form of the word, and regardless of how many times I've been hurt in friendship, I love people and I am a good friend.

So let's get out of our own way by choosing to allow the hard times to bring us back to our core, shake off all the things that are weighing us down and strengthen what remains.

Who Am I?

There are the voices that have challenged our identity and worth and then there are those things in our lives that have been passed down from generation to generation. Some of them we like, and some . . . not so much. I have my mother's hips and gave them to my girls too. My oldest won't let me live it down, as if I had demanded that she receive this inheritance. In addition to the hips, my mom gave me ample cushion on the posterior end, if you know what I mean.

I'll never forget one Christmas at my grandmother's house when my uncle gathered everyone around in the living room of her manufactured home. We were like sardines, but we didn't care. He stood there with a captive audience and began his speech, "I love all of you Snyder women, and there's one thing you all have in common. I'm dedicating this song to you today." He hit play and the lyrics began, "She's got a butt bigger than the Beatles. . . . " My grandmother was barely five feet tall, and I have never seen her move so fast! She jumped up, ran across the room and tackled my six-foot uncle to the ground. I've never laughed so hard in my life.

So we all have them (not the crazy family, although we all have those too . . .): things that have been passed down from generation to generation, things that hurt us growing up, things we can't change about ourselves without winning the lottery, and things that completely changed our trajectory whether for the good or for the bad. We often get hung up on these things, thinking that we can't do anything to change them so we just accept the same repetitive failures that have been modeled for us. While inheriting burdensome hips, the women in my family have seen the redeeming power of Christ crushing crippling patterns of pain, such as teen pregnancy and divorce, demonstrating that with God's help we can break unhealthy generational patterns.

Taking it further, I believe that a difficult history can make you the greatest wife, parent, teacher, minister, counselor or friend. You can be more compassionate because you understand how it feels. You can be more patient because you know the challenge. You can be more discerning because you are aware of the spiritual aspects of the struggle.

For example, when I started to homeschool my son during his seventh-grade year, I caught him cheating. In fact, I uncovered several spelling tests that he had cheated on. I knew he had cheated, I knew the lie he would tell me when I confronted him and I knew all of his internal struggles that led him to his decision to cheat in the first place. I knew them before he said a word. How? Because guess who was homeschooled and cheated on her spelling test? This girl!

I told him, "Son, there's nothing that you can do that will get by me, because I've done it all!" I was able to not just speak to the cheating, but I also spoke to the deeper things that were going on in his heart. (And don't worry, the punishment fit the crime. Don't be the parent that just deals with heart issues and doesn't punish the wrongdoing. To withhold discipline from a child is to say you don't love them, and you don't care about their future.) We were closer after this moment, our conversations became deeper, and so much more honesty was born because I knew what to do. I knew what I needed when it was me, and I was a better mother for it.

We can have natural outcomes, or we can have redeemed outcomes.

The point is that all life hardships develop you, but how have you let them shape you? Think about it. We can have natural outcomes, or we can have redeemed outcomes, like we've talked about with Rahab. The choice is ours.

There are people I've known that grew up in the home of someone who was an alcoholic, and they won't even have a casual, occasional drink because they never wanted to fall into the trap of addiction. I've also known people that have been in the same situation, and they just repeated what they saw, never striving for more for themselves. Learn to appreciate all that has developed you, including the pain, life's lessons, disappointments, promotions, relationships, mentorship and the Holy Spirit. What was doesn't have to be what is.

Rahab could have said, "I am a prostitute,"
but instead her life said, *"I am in the lineage of Christ."*
Ester could have said, "I am an orphan,"
but instead her life said, *"I am a queen."*
Deborah could have said, "I am barren,"
but instead her life said, *"I am a mother to Israel."*
David could have said, "I am a murderer,"
but instead his life said, *"I am God's chosen."*
Joshua could have said "I am a slave,"
but instead his life said, *"I am a deliverer."*
What will you say?

Often we blame or deny the past, but rarely do we see that all things will be used to make us, but who we become is completely up to us. Our circumstances alone cannot make us, our mistakes can't

Don't allow the trauma that has happened in your life dictate the trajectory of your life.

make us—we choose if we will use them or if we will be used by them! Don't allow the trauma that has happened in your life dictate the trajectory of your life. Let me tell you this, where we are is not who we are. You may find yourself in the worst place you have ever been, but that does not define you. We are in the process of becoming and your prison-like situation can be your place of preparation. Like Joseph, you can just be doing your time, and in one swift move from God, you can become the second in command. God's got more in you and for you. Lean in and remember who you are.

Overcome

To be true to who you are, you can't let life's struggles get you down and define you. We've been studying Joshua, and he had plenty of moments where I'm sure he thought, "Is this all my life is going to boil down to?" but yet he overcame. He was true to the person God created him to be and didn't allow the voices of the world to drown out his identity in Christ; in fact, he allowed the difficulties of life to be a teacher to him. He used pain as his tool to overcome doubt, fear, regret, rejection and so much more.

Joshua was born in slavery, poverty, oppression, and yet it taught him how to pray. His whole life he was taught to be subservient, but around forty years of age, he was set free and promoted by God as leader of the armies of Israel. That's hope for us forty-somethings! Every ounce of oppression that was put on him from birth was now used for righteous anger, and he led Israel to victory after victory.

Joshua was in the minority in Israel as one of two who gave a good report on the Promised Land. He was rejected by his own people. They wanted to stone him, yet he didn't run. He learned how to have staying capacity during a season any of us would have wanted to retreat! He outlasted those who hated him and led their children forty years later into the land they had rejected. If there's one thing I've learned in ministry it's you've got to outlast the negative voices that are around you. In due time God will set things straight, but in the meantime, keep showing up. Make the enemy eat his words!

In due time God will set things straight, but in the meantime, keep showing up.

Joshua experienced delay after delay in his life, even though they weren't all caused by him, but it taught him to be patient, to seek God, to obey God, to trust God, and ultimately, it taught him how to lead. I don't know about you, but I sometimes get frustrated with people. I would not have been good in the wilderness, because I'm the kind of person that gets stuff done. The circling would have driven me crazy! In times like these, I have to remind myself of the words in 2 Peter 3:15 (AMP): "And consider the patience of our Lord [His delay in judging and avenging wrongs] as salvation [that is, allowing time for more to be saved]."

It's literally the patience of the Lord that has afforded me my salvation! There's no way my name would be in the Lamb's Book of Life (the reservation book to enter heaven) if it had not been for the patience of God that pursued me even in my rebellion!

Joshua didn't try to lead like Moses, he learned from Moses. Joshua sent out two spies, not twelve. In the battle of Ai, he extended his arm, and unlike Moses in the battle with the Amalekites, he didn't get tired, withdraw or take a seat. He knew what it felt like to be the guy on the battlefield, and he had a tenacity about him that pushed him to do better, be better, fight harder and see his people to victory. Joshua was the man for the job.

He used every experience in his life to build. He built others. He built his own heart. He built his relationship with the Lord. He built his trust. Joshua lived an overcoming life through God's redeeming hand. Joshua's name is derived from the Hebrew name "Yehoshua," meaning "God is deliverance."[15] God did not name Joshua "slave" or any other label the world tried to pin on him, He named him deliverance because that's exactly what God intended to do when the world would attempt to steal his identity. He lived his true name in Christ. He lived delivered! Similarly, Jesus's name is derived from the Hebrew name "Yeshua," meaning "God is salvation."[16] Because Jesus saves, we too can live delivered. Jesus has rescued us and stores up unimaginable blessings for our future.

Jesus paid a high price for us to gain.

Jesus paid a high price for us to gain. When the enemy works against you, make him pay by using everything to learn to become who God has called you to be! Whatever your background, no matter the abuse you've endured, the critical words you experienced, the losses that hit you, God can still mold you into a strong vessel, beautiful and powerful for what He has in mind!

> *But we have this treasure in jars of clay to show that this all-surpassing power is from God and not from us. We are hard pressed on every side, but not crushed; perplexed, but not in despair; persecuted, but not abandoned; struck down, but not destroyed.*
> *2 Corinthians 4:7 (NIV)*

You are a treasure. Be brave. *Be you.*

"To be prepared for war is one of the most effective means of preserving peace."

-George Washington

Be on your guard; stand firm in the faith; be courageous; be strong.

1 Corinthians 16:13 (NIV)

Chapter 12
Be Alert

We can't always foresee life's moments of difficulty, but as discussed in chapter 4, creating healthy spiritual habits can carry us through some of the most difficult times. We tend to only go to God when we are bleeding, but don't take care of our spiritual health up until that point or after. It's hard mentally to be disciplined when you feel like you're doing OK, as other things naturally take precedence. I don't feel I need to go to the gym until I try on a bathing suit. However, our health is important all year, right? So is our spiritual health!

If you haven't figured it out just yet, being a Christian doesn't make your problems go away. So our spiritual health is vital to our success here on Earth. God doesn't want to be your urgent care clinic or ER visit. He wants a relationship with you. Likewise, I don't want to use God, I want to have a relationship with Him. When my relationship is strong, even when I'm hit by life, I'm stronger and more prepared for the battle I'm facing.

When we align our beliefs with our daily lifestyles, we actually begin to live out what we believe. What would happen if all of us began to practice what we preach? Our faith would go from head knowledge to a life of strong conviction and profound outcomes.

Sober

*Be sober [well balanced and self-disciplined],
be alert and cautious at all times. That enemy of yours,
the devil, prowls around like a roaring lion [fiercely
hungry], seeking someone to devour.*
1 Peter 5:8 (AMP)

When we think of the word sober, we often contrast it with a drunken state, but this word of caution from the scripture means something completely different to me. When I've just been victorious, although I'm excited and spiritually energized, I am also completely physically drained. Think about a runner finishing their race. When they get done, they want to eat, rehydrate and sleep off the victory. It's not the time to go out for another physically exhausting activity. It's the same spiritually. When we have been in a fight, power has gone out of us, and we need to be refreshed in the Lord to create balance and order. In an exhausted state, our caution can lower, and it's likely that our vision will be clouded. To be sober spiritually requires us to be self-disciplined, not let things slide and be alert at all times.

I have some of the most amazing faith-filled women in my life that challenge me to not just read the Word of God but to embody the Spirit of Christ at all times. It's fascinating to see how being around people of great faith encourages and enlarges our own faith! One particular friend of mine had been meditating on this scripture: *Very truly I tell you, whoever believes in me will do the works I have been doing, and they will do even greater things than these, because I am going to the Father* John 14:12 (NIV).

> *Being around people of great faith encourages and enlarges our own faith!*

Her prayer was to follow Christ's example and Word to us. She had seen many healings and spiritual breakthroughs throughout her life but had never seen anyone raised from the dead, which Jesus was known to do from time to time. She boldly and specifically began to pray that God would give her the courage and faith to see such a miracle work through her life.

One night on her shift as a neonatal nurse, her panicked colleague called for her to come help her with a patient. Her team knew she was a Christian, and they needed something that went way beyond their nursing skills. A sweet baby girl had been stillborn, and the mother was hysterical, as any mother would be. My friend walked into the room and the Holy Spirit took over. She grabbed the mom, looked her in the eye and said, "Do you want to see your child live?" The mother responded, "Yes." She urged her, "Then pray with me." She believed for the sweet girl to be brought back from death's doors, and within minutes, the Lord answered their prayers as this infant took her first breath.

It was a glorious moment for everyone in the room, especially my friend who had more than one prayer answered that night! I can't even imagine the relief that the mother experienced as she held her baby girl, who went from death to life. There is no doubt that God has a great purpose for her.

The next day, my friend left for vacation on a high note, knowing Christ even more intimately than before. When she returned, she inquired about the baby to the other nurses to see how she was doing. They let her know that they had to transfer her to another hospital because she had been documented as dead for so long, they wanted to ensure there was no brain damage. She and the other nurses excitedly called up the hospital to get an update.

Shocked, the nurse hung up the phone and was saddened to share that the girl had died. Bewildered and yet defiant of the news, my friend said, "Call them again and double-check." The nurse obliged and kindly asked the hospital to double-check the records, and when they did, they said, "I'm sorry. We were looking at the wrong file. The baby had no additional injuries and was released completely healthy and strong!"

Excuse me for a moment while I happy dance. When my friend told me this story, I envisioned a cartoon red devil version of Satan holding what he thinks will be a winning hand, but then my friend called his bluff with a royal flush! BAM! Listen to me, even when you have a victory, the enemy will try to steal your confidence. This little girl was healed and alive no matter what my friend believed, but if she had not called the enemy's bluff, her confidence could have been shaken. It's possible that her next encounter with a need may have been met with caution and doubt instead of faith. Challenge the lies that are handed to you, and be alert that the enemy is a thief always looking for what he can steal. Don't make it easy for him by believing what he says so easily.

After every victory I have, I almost immediately have an attack that comes in the form of a lie, accusation or an invitation to meditate on things I could have done better, as if the victory was because of me anyway. The victory is the Lord's. When it comes, thank Him for it and don't allow the enemy to have any part in it. I've come to expect these assaults, and now I can recognize them and work to silence them instead of entertaining them! You should too.

You must remain sober to silence them. To put it plain and simple, the enemy attacks when we are tired in hopes of discouraging us. I have three kids, and there have been times when I've been so physically exhausted that I just didn't care that they were about to kill each other. I just let them go at it and buried my head in a pillow. But, eventually, I would wake up to the mess and just feel defeated. It's these debilitating moments that discourage us. We are supposed to fight for victory, but we can't do that if we are exhausted and discouraged.

It's impossible to just push past fatigue. We have to take the appropriate rest needed to replenish. After years in the ministry, my husband and I have discovered the importance of recharging after seasons we know are going to require a spiritual fight and physical exhaustion. Looking at our calendar, we will plan time off after big events to give us time for rest and reflection. Additionally, in seasons of hardship, we have taken the appropriate time of rest to heal.

Jesus modeled this so well. Over and over in the New Testament, you see Him minister to large crowds, perform healings and miracles and then retreat to connect with His Father, to rest and realign.

You may not be resting because you are performing.

At times, we are not resting because we are performing. We chase the next high to fill our identity tank with the praise of people, but it just leaves us depleted and vain. Jesus never got His worth mixed up in the praise of people, what He did, how many people showed up or the offering given. He knew who He was. He had a sober mind. A sober mind keeps us alert, detecting these false fillers and renewing our purpose through a departure of shallow activity and purposeful solitude with the Lord.

Fraud

The enemy wants to steal what you've gained, and if he can't do that, he'll settle for challenging your identity, getting you to question who you are. Out of the blue, I received a text message from my bank saying that there was some suspicious activity on my account. I was instructed to review the charges and either confirm or deny them. I looked, and one of the payments was made to HEB, our local grocery store, and for a minute I thought, "I go to HEB. It could have been me." Upon further investigation, I realized that the charge was in a different city altogether.

The enemy loves to fill you with fraudulent thoughts. We must be alert to investigate those thoughts.

I think it's possible when we are going through difficulty or victory that we think things like:

- ♥ Maybe I deserve this.
- ♥ This is all my fault.
- ♥ God isn't in this with me.
- ♥ Things are always going to be stacked against me.
- ♥ There's no hope.
- ♥ No one would understand.

Or even:

- ♥ I'm really amazing.
- ♥ I accomplished this all on my own.
- ♥ Look at everyone around me and how they hang on my every word.

The enemy wants you to confirm these allegations, but there's been fraudulent activity on your account! Revelations 12:10 says that the enemy accuses us day and night, but it also says that the accuser has been cast down through the power of Jesus Christ.

For a moment, as I reviewed the amounts in question, I doubted my whereabouts, my purchases, my involvement, but then I came to my senses. I want you to come to your senses and do what I did. I picked up my phone and said, "Charges denied!" I canceled my card and nothing touched my bank account. Cancel the lies. You have access to unlimited resources because you have an unlimited God that loves you! Don't get a hold put on your account. It's because God loves you that you aren't going to get what you deserve, you're going to get Christ's love, forgiveness and His faithfulness. There's hope, there's healing, there's life no matter what accusations have been brought against you.

You have access to unlimited resources because you have an unlimited God that loves you!

Be alert. The enemy wants to steal. You must fiercely protect your identity. Know your whereabouts. Where am I in my thinking? Where am I in my attitude? Where am I in my heart? Where am I in the Word of God? Where am I in the house of God? Where am I in my calling? Where am I in my relationships? The enemy will bring a charge against you, but if you cannot clearly recognize it as fraud, you will accept it and pay for it.

You must fiercely protect your identity.

Deception

I hate deception. There is a card game my kids like to play where you can lie about the characters you've been dealt. I cannot stand to play it because lying, manipulating and any form of deception offends my spirit, even if it's just a game. Satan has been a master schemer since before the beginning of time. He hates all that is good, pure and true, which is why it would be advantageous for us to carefully weigh things that are brought before us by measuring them according to the Word of God and bringing them before the Lord in prayer.

For example, if someone at work asks us to push something through for their benefit, but it would hurt the company or cause us to have to lie or be deceitful, we can find the answer in Leviticus 19:11: *Do not steal. Do not lie. Do not deceive one another* (NIV).

By going to the Word, we can have clarity on how we should respond in order to honor God and keep our identity secured in Him. If you have a more complex issue and don't feel like you can find a black and white answer to the situation in the Word, you can first take it to prayer. By waiting on the Lord, He can give you peace regarding the direction you should go. Likewise, asking for wise counsel provides deeper guidance, affirming what we sense the Lord is desiring us to do. Out of the mouths of two or three different people, we can be secure in our decision (2 Corinthians 13:1). It's also possible that the right people will see impending danger, not the roses you want them to see around the decision you desire to make, and that's OK. We stay neutral in what we want, so we can see what God wants. Consult with people who love God and love you enough to counsel you with the truth, whether or not it's something you want to hear. These methods will save us all a lot of heartaches if we can learn to put them to practice.

These are all teachings I think Joshua would have given us himself if he were still with us, but we can still certainly learn from his mistakes. At times, Joshua would consult God and experience victory, and at other times, he would suffer by making his own plans. It seemed that after every win, he'd also experience a deception. Let's see how Joshua handled it:

> *However, when the people of Gibeon heard what Joshua had done to Jericho and Ai, they resorted to a ruse: They went as a delegation whose donkeys were loaded with worn-out sacks and old wineskins, cracked and mended. They put worn and patched sandals on their feet and wore old clothes. All the bread of their food supply was dry and moldy. Then they went to Joshua in the camp at Gilgal and said to him and the Israelites, "We have come from a distant country; make a treaty with us." Joshua 9:3-6 (NIV)*

The cunning Gibeonites resorted to a great deception, and I have to say it was pretty elementary. I wonder if they had tryouts for who would act out each role before they sent them off to deliver this Emmy award-winning performance. Nevertheless, Joshua and his leadership team completely fell for it:

> *The Israelites sampled their provisions but did not inquire of the Lord. Then Joshua made a treaty of peace with them to let them live, and the leaders of the assembly ratified it by oath. Joshua 9:14-15 (NIV)*

Joshua had a victory at Jericho and Ai, but now encountered another decision after an exhausting feat. Do you see a pattern?

Battle of Jericho→	Consulted God→	Win
Achan's Hidden Sin→	Deception→	Defeat
Second Battle of Ai→	Consulted God→	Win
Gibeon's Encounter→	Deception→	Defeat

Israel instinctively knew something was off with the Gibeonite story, but instead of consulting the One who could give them clear instruction, even when they were tired, they bypassed their safety and their help in the Lord for their own convenience. When we take shortcuts, we always pay a great price. It's better to take your time and be sure than to rush into something and not have included God in the process. It took all of three days for the deception to be brought to light, as Israel discovered that Gibeon was actually a neighboring town, not a faraway city that they had journeyed from.

For Christmas one year, we bought my son a basketball hoop. He was so excited for us to put it together, and we were excited to give it to him, but not excited to put it together. The YouTube tutorials warned us that it would take a minimum of four hours with two people putting it together. I tried very hard to get my husband to utilize the family we had in town to accomplish this task, but no, he waited until it was just him and me to have this bonding experience. After a few days and many hours (more than four), we finally had it put together, and I use the term "we" loosely because my husband did most of the heavy lifting. The only problem with it was that it leaned. After carefully looking over the engineering, I thought that I had located the problem. One of the initial support poles looked like it was placed backward.

My husband insisted it was placed correctly because he had thoroughly read the directions, and he remembered reading that all the instructional stickers on the poles were to face the outward direction. I left him alone to do some additional investigation. When I came back, he hung his head and said, "You were right. They must have put the label on incorrectly." He then confessed to having to beat the poles to be able to fit them into one another, as it was "almost impossible to get them to go together" . . . because they weren't supposed to be put together! That should have been the first red flag that something wasn't right. So that basketball hoop sat there, crooked and unused for quite some time. I hate being right.

If it doesn't feel right, if you're forcing it, stop! Take a moment to invite the Holy Spirit into your decision-making process. So much can change in three days. Just ask Jesus! It's OK to pause and wait. Israel was so furious with its leadership for falling for this ruse. I can imagine the cold shoulders and toxic chatter of the people as Joshua and his team walked humiliated by their careless decision that resulted in a loss of land for their community.

If it doesn't feel right, if you're forcing it, stop!

Gibeon would have been their next conquest, but now they had made a treaty with them in front of the Lord, which made it binding. They brought God into the close of the deal but left him out of the process from start to finish. God can redeem all things, but when we bring Jesus in only at the finish line, we are surely going to have consequences. I don't know about you, but I want my all-knowing God to be counseling me in every transaction from beginning to end, from start to finish.

What decision in your life can you look back on and realize you did not inquire of the Lord? The enemy is counting on you to exclude God from time to time. He's looking for that right opportunity to pounce on you with the hopes that he will derail you, but remember that even though we may have messed up, God is the redeemer of all things and will find a way to turn things around when we truly repent for our faults.

The Lord Fights for Us

In Joshua 10, you will discover that Gibeon was a very important city in that region, due to its size, and all of its men were incredible fighters. The neighboring cities decided to ban together to take Israel and Gibeon out for good, but they forgot one thing: when God is on your side, nothing formed against you will prosper. The Lord encouraged Joshua and assured him that they had the victory. They took them by surprise, and Israel used all the advantages they had through the Lord's plan. God threw the enemy into confusion, and they defeated their enemy in the city of Gibeon. Now that's called a comeback:

*As they fled before Israel on the road down from
Beth Horon to Azekah, the Lord hurled large hailstones
down on them, and more of them died from the hail
than were killed by the swords of the Israelites.
On the day the Lord gave the Amorites over to Israel, Joshua
said to the Lord in the presence of Israel:
"Sun, stand still over Gibeon,
and you, moon, over the Valley of Aijalon."
So the sun stood still,
and the moon stopped,
till the nation avenged itself on its enemies,
as it is written in the Book of Jashar.
The sun stopped in the middle of the sky and delayed going
down about a full day. There has never been a day like it before
or since, a day when the Lord listened to a human being.
Surely the Lord was fighting for Israel!
Joshua 10:11-14 (NIV)*

Joshua invited God to take His rightful lead as Father and defender of Israel. More of Israel's adversaries were killed by the hailstorm God sent than by the swords of one of the most powerful armies on Earth. Make a note to yourself, no matter how powerful or successful we become, it's minuscule in comparison to who our God is. So let's surrender and let God take the lead. He will take out our enemies in ways we never could.

At times, it can feel like we are fighting a battle that is doomed, hope can seem lost and fears can slow down our progress. Joshua had many wins and losses over the course of his life, but he didn't stop fighting until he had complete victory. Today is the only day that matters, so set your heart on daily victories so you can endure the length of the battle. Today, you can have a victory in your heart. You can have victory in your prayer life. You can have victory in your diet. You can have victory in your mind. You can mend a relationship, you can choose to spend time with God, you can go an extra mile.

Today you can because God will!

Today you can because God will! Joshua knew nothing was too small or too great that the Lord could not take care of it. Joshua let the Lord fight for him by asking God to do things only God can do.

When Joshua commanded the sun to stand still, he invited the light to shine until the darkness was completely overtaken. Light can be a little overwhelming to our systems after being in darkness. When I get up in the morning, the last thing I want is to have a bright light shining on my face, but the more awake I become, the more the light serves me and helps me make the right decisions, go the right direction and address anything that might be out of order or out of place. God has called us to live awake, in the light, sober-minded, alert and readied for success. Invite the light in, draw back the shades, open the curtains and hide nothing from the presence of God! Be alert.

Operating in Authority

When the light comes on, we are empowered to move with confidence, alert and awakened with clear sight. The boldness on Joshua's life was undeniable when he commanded the sun to stay still. It was with full confidence that Joshua spoke as a son to the sun, and by the Son of God, it was done. We have authority in our sonship!

So you are no longer a slave, but God's child; and
since you are his child, God has made you also an heir.
Galatians 4:7 (NIV)

Joshua went from slave to son. When we come into a relationship with Jesus, we go from slave to sin to daughter of Christ. As daughters, we are heirs, continuing the legacy of faith that Jesus began and imparted to us.

Jesus spoke the world into motion and, in doing so, taught us that our words hold power. Power to hurt. Power to heal. Power to produce miracles. Being alert to the gifts of God helps us to operate in authority as children of God. It was Jesus himself who said that we who believe in Him will do even greater things than what He did! When was the last time you exercised your authority in Christ to see these great things accomplished? If Christ gave you authority and you never exercise it, I think it's time to ask yourself why. To have authority and not use it suggests a mindset of bondage. It's like me living in a house that is fully capable of using electricity but refusing to turn on the light. My granny once ruined a dishwasher by not running it in an effort to preserve it. As daughters in Christ, we are legally entitled to operate in authority, but when we surrender or yield our authority to darkness, we freely and legally give authority for the enemy to operate. Be alert to not give away what God meant for you to use for His glory.

Spiritual authority has nothing to do with what we have to offer, it has to do with the Father and our relationship and obedience to Him. When you are a kid, the more obedient to your parents you are, the more your parents trust you and give you more freedom and responsibility. Likewise, God as our spiritual Father gives us more authority when we are obedient and observant to His laws, His ways and His prompting.

Years ago, I was in the kitchen cleaning up after dinner. My pre-teen daughter was unhappy that I had told her to go get her laundry from upstairs and put it in the washer. She turned, stomped off and began sulking her way to her room. She didn't get very far when I called her back not once but twice to work on her less than joyful behavior that was revealing itself through her expressive body language. Finally, she got it right, but she doubled the time that it took.

The next time I asked her to do something, she did it quickly and with a great attitude, and even better than that, I don't even have to ask her to do her laundry anymore. She does it on her own without prompting. When I see her character grow, I want to give her more privileges and responsibility and trust is authored between us. God wants us to grow in our obedience to Him, and as a result, we activate the authority we have as believers, and we can see what God wants us to do. If we really believe that He will do what He says he will do, why wouldn't we move quickly and joyfully when approached with opportunities for the miracles of God to answer the problems of life?

God will ask us to do things that we will not understand. We will walk through seasons that aren't comfortable for us, and that's OK because the enemy of Christianity is ease. Traveling to many places in the world makes you aware that our freedoms in our westernized culture have wastefully been spent on living comfortable lives. We've let our guard down, being drunk on lavish lifestyles.

The enemy of Christianity is ease.

What's worse is that what we have is never enough. We want more, bigger, newer, but all of the things that we think will lead to a life of ease instead deliver an incessant need for more. There is nothing easy about Christianity, but there is nothing more fulfilling than a life truly lived in step with Christ. God did not send His Son to this earth on a private jet, He was born in the most awkward of circumstances, in the dirtiest of places, and in the same manner, He asks of us to take awkward steps toward His voice, choosing to be alert to His desires not our own.

Jesus did weird things sometimes. I would have certainly chosen a more dignified way to heal people than spitting on them, putting mud on their eyes, waiting days after they've died to heal them and bring their stinky corpse out of the grave, and that's just to name a few. If God is to get the glory, then we have to be willing to go from comfortable to plain old awkward. Think of how Joshua must have felt walking around the walls of Jericho over and over and over and over and over until finally, the walls fell in. People may just think you are plum crazy for the things that God asks you to do. In the end, it doesn't matter what people think. When we're obedient,

Jesus delivers on His promises and no one can deny His power. As we stretch and are willing to just do what He says, our confidence grows in knowing that we hear God and that He will come through on His Word.

Do I battle with doubt? You bet! Many times when I've exercised authority in Christ, I've had some level of doubt that tries to creep in, but I do it anyway. Just like exercising a muscle, authority grows with continued engagement and weight. In Matthew 17, it talks about having faith the size of a mustard seed and that, even at that tiny state, when activated, it can move mountains. In Matthew 13, we get a bigger picture of the mustard seed and learn that although it may be the smaller of the seeds, when fully grown, it is larger than the other garden plants, and it becomes a tree.

I was speaking at a conference, and during a time of prayer for healing, the Lord gave me a word of knowledge so I spoke it. There was an issue with someone's jaw, but I didn't know who. As I prayed I commanded the pain to leave in the name of Jesus. Afterward, I wondered if anything had happened. About three weeks later, a gentleman ran into me at church and said that he had been wanting to talk to me. He shared that his wife was at the conference and had dislocated her jaw and had been in continual pain because of it. I had asked anyone with pain to stand, but she didn't stand because she thought her need was too small compared to the other needs in the room. When I spoke, the pain immediately left her body and she wept that God saw her and cared about what she was going through. I told her husband that this act of healing from Christ was to grow her faith because there would be bigger things down the road, and the Lord wanted them to believe, knowing that He cares about the details of their lives. Just a few months later he shared with me that because of a cancer battle, the doctors had told him he would never have kids. Then he pulled out his phone and showed me a beautiful sonogram of their sweet miracle baby. God cares about the details of our lives!

I can't say this enough: spiritual authority is not about our power, it's about the power of Christ and the depth of our trust in His Word. All believers have been given authority through Christ, but it's up to us to practice using it for God's glory. With the authority given to us, let's also recognize the great responsibility we have to steward it. A lack of authority equals chaos. Just ask my kids. If I leave them alone and don't designate someone to be in charge, chaos ensues! Look at what has happened through movements to get rid of police officers and at cities that refused to hold looters accountable for their actions. Their cities became desolate, lawless and left begging for support.

Not using our authority in Christ equals suffering for others.

This world is full of confusion, but what if we, as believers, stepped up to the plate and started to move mountains, break barriers and heal the hurting; what could happen? It's demoralizing to have been given responsibility without the authority to accomplish the task given, but what about when we have the authority and we take no responsibility? As Christians we have been given authority and often we aren't taking responsibility to operate in it! How many people around us are suffering because we won't walk in the gifts that God has given us?

I want to have such a relationship with my heavenly Father that He listens to me when I ask Him for naturally impossible things. God knows my heart, my character and my endurance to see what He wants done accomplished, and likewise, I know that my obedience partnered with His power will accomplish His will. The issue lies when we decide to pick up the spirit of fear instead of the Spirit of Christ. When was the last time you asked God for something humanly impossible?

It seems silly looking back on it, but at the time, it had our full attention. My husband and I were going to a church conference where we would minister and be ministered to. Our first flight was delayed, which made our connecting flight tight. We got off the plane and ran to a terminal across the airport. Neither of us are runners, which made for an interesting sight. We arrived at the gate completely out of breath. The plane was still there, but they had closed the doors.

If you know anything about flying, you know that once they close the doors you aren't getting on that flight! The paperwork has been completed, and there is no hope left. We approached the desk anyway and the stewardess let us know that we would have to look for another flight. We sat down, and my husband began to tweet, but I began to pray. "Lord, you can move mountains. I can see this plane, and I believe you can open the doors for us." Within minutes, the stewardess came over to us and said, "The pilot has instructed us to open the doors for you." She had shock in her eyes as she was sharing this with us. My husband looked at me, and I said, "While you were tweeting, I was praying."

The Lord will do much greater things than this, but the point is that God hears you. He fights our fights and opens up our flights! He's for you. He wants you to *God fights our fights and opens up our flights!* ask Him for the sun to stand still in your situation. There's a miracle that is hanging in the balance of you coming into alignment with what God wants and confidently requesting our Father to do the impossible. Speak with the authority God's given you, and do not be deceived by the circumstances you face or the voice that incessantly comes against you. You are made for more. *Be alert,* friend.

My Reflections

"The adventure of a Christian life begins when we dare to do what we would never tackle without Christ."

–William Penn

I will give you every place where you set your foot, as I promised Moses.

Joshua 1:3 (NIV)

Chapter 13
Be Adventurous

Unfortunately, Moses would never set foot in the Promised Land on this side of eternity. It's a very sobering thought that someone of Moses's faith and conquest would stop short of his dream. When wildfire fears were spread by ten of the twelve spies, God responded to their disbelief in a way that has sobered my view of the choices I face: *As for your children that you said would be taken as plunder, I will bring them in to enjoy the land you have rejected.* Numbers 14:31 (NIV)

When I read this scripture, my heart was heavy with this question: What has God tried to give me to enjoy that I've rejected? To enjoy means to take delight or pleasure in or to possess and benefit from,[17] whereas to reject something means to refuse to agree.[18] In essence, we'd rather refuse to agree with God than to take pleasure and benefit from Him.

Instead of embracing a life of adventure, Israel accepted fear and rejected prosperity. How often are we rejecting the goodness of God for the wildfire fears of this world? When looking at fear and prosperity side by side, I'd choose prosperity all day every day, but fear is so much louder and more enticing than God's promises because His promises will always demand a step of faith for us to inhabit. God's promises require us to see what He sees, and we won't be able to see what God sees from a natural perspective, so we have to look at things through a supernatural lens.

For a moment, think about things in your life you have rejected, but in hindsight, you realize God sent them to you for you to enjoy. In doing this exercise myself, I've realized, as you have already read, that in past seasons, I have rejected myself. God created me to enjoy who I am in Him, but I have looked in the mirror and torn myself apart for how I look, how I think, what I have or what I don't have. That was never God's intent when He fashioned me. God wants us to be comfortable in our own skin and to enjoy all the things that make us unique.

My list of rejections goes on:

- ♥ I have rejected my calling at times because I didn't feel qualified.
- ♥ I have rejected love because I didn't feel lovable.
- ♥ I have rejected friendship because I had been hurt.
- ♥ I have rejected feedback because of insecurity.
- ♥ I have rejected healing because I couldn't face the truth.

This is going to be an ouch statement: someone is enjoying what you've rejected. There may have been a job someone else is enjoying because you didn't feel qualified enough to accept it. Potentially, there are scholarships you didn't apply for because of fear of rejection, and another who took a risk is enjoying them. There are friends you wouldn't trust that are being enjoyed by an accepting soul.

Someone is enjoying what you've rejected.

Some of my closest friends that I enjoy the most were rejected by their families. One of my best friends was rejected by her father, and even though they live in the same town, he has never once tried to meet her or acknowledge her presence. He looked at his choices all wrong when he found out she was coming into the world. All he saw was responsibility and a tarnished reputation, but he had no idea what a delight she would become. When God fashioned her, He took the best parts of her dad and mixed them with the wholehearted goodness of her mother. Her generous spirit and overwhelming joy enter every room with her, and her dad missed it! He rejected what God sent him to enjoy.

Another friend of mine rejected her boyfriend for years. Every time he'd propose, she'd say no. Her history of experiencing a lot of pain got in the way of her adventurous outlook on her future. Her ex-husband had committed suicide, and a few years later, so did her son. The pain was excruciating and the thought of losing another man that she loved was too much to bear, but she was looking at her choice all wrong. God wasn't giving her something to lose, He was giving her someone to enjoy! God began to heal her through her commitment to

Small Groups, and I am happy to tell you that she has been married for several years now! This is why community is so incredibly important to our future! Let's be women who ignite faith and healing, not fear. She walked into the promise of God and said, "I do!" and has from that moment forward enjoyed a life of adventure in a marriage that she had once rejected!

The choice seems easy side by side:

- ♥ Hurt or Healing
- ♥ Friendship or Loneliness
- ♥ Humility or Humiliation
- ♥ Hero or Coward

However, when you let your history rule your future, you'll be hitting the reject button all day every day. It takes faith to enjoy what God's giving you!

Now faith is confidence in what we hope
for and assurance about what we do not see.
Hebrews 11:1 (NIV)

Let's not miss out on the adventure of a lifetime because of fear. In order for us to make the right choice, an action is required on our end of things.

Cheap Seat

Most of the adventures I've experienced in life have had an aircraft involved in them. Whether I was exploring the lustrous colors of the Amalfi Coast or ministering in the dirt-ridden heat of the Bush in Africa, a plane took me there. However, one particular trip and plane made for a lot more nerves than excitement.

My husband had wanted to go skydiving for his birthday, so of course, I took him to a beautiful facility, where the gear was pristine, the instructors were professional and the planes were well maintained. They had detailed instruction videos to show you everything you could expect and to prepare you for all of the safety measures. At the time, I didn't really think anything of it. We spared no expense, and he had an unforgettable adventure.

Have you ever heard the old saying, "You get what you pay for!"? Well, my sister-in-law and I learned that the hard way. We both love to find a deal, so what did we do when we decided we wanted to go skydiving? We found a coupon! While I had spared no expense for my husband, I cheaped out for myself.

As women, we can find ourselves pouring into others, sparing no expense, but when it comes to our own health, needs, spirituality and desires, we cheap out!

Our skydiving trip was different than my husband's. As we drove up, our eyes were a little stunned that there was no nice building; it was a trailer park. There were no friendly people to meet us and answer our questions. There weren't skydiving suits for us to put over our clothes. The gear was tattered; in fact, after we jumped, my tandem instructor informed me that they had brought him in from out of state to try to help bring them up to code and then he proceeded to show me all of the equipment that was broken on his suit that we just jumped with! Don't even get me started on the plane. It looked like it came from a rescue mission out of the Vietnam War! I'm surprised that it made it up to the 12,000 feet required for the jump!

At that point, the air seemed much safer than the aircraft itself! My feet were dangling out of the beat-up four-seater plane where the back two seats had been ripped out, and there was literally duct tape covering the holes. There were several distinct thoughts that raced through my head, like "Why did you choose the cheapest place to do the most deadly thing you could ever do?" My appetite to chase adventure, all while saving a buck, began to haunt me! Just like that, in those fleeting seconds, we dove out of the aircraft, and prayerfully and thankfully, we landed safely on solid ground!

Have you ever had a "What was I thinking?" moment? Have you ever taken the cheapest way to do something that could so drastically impact your life or the life of others? There are moments in our Christian walk that define the richness of our relationship with Christ. Moments where we step out in faith or draw back in fear. Moments where we give all we have or turn a blind eye to problems we could so easily be an answer to. Moments where we take a leap or we retreat. Moments where we will stand with unshaken confidence or we will embrace cheap lies about who we are.

I want to live these moments out with my eyes wide open, having not one ounce of regret, seeing every opportunity for

God's Word to come alive and seizing every moment to put belief to action.

Your eyes are windows into your body. If you
open your eyes wide in wonder and belief, your body fills
up with light. If you live squinty-eyed in greed and distrust,
your body is a dank cellar. If you pull the blinds on
your windows, what a dark life you will have!
Matthew 6:22-23 (MSG)

I'm not taking the cheap seat of fear. I am not sitting in the back of the plane because I don't think I have what it takes to ride first class. I'm not going to hold tight to the wings of insecurity. I'm not going to sit at the terminal of complacency, having dreams but never taking a risk. I refuse to take the cheap seat of doubt, questioning God at his every move and change in direction. I won't put the mask on someone else before I first get the breath of life pumping through my being. I won't let my health deteriorate because I'm afraid of what the doctor will say or because I don't want to face a diagnosis. I am a first-class girl when it comes to adventure! I've learned my lesson. How about you?

You might be wondering what kind of trip God wants to take you on. Jesus gave his disciples direction that will take you where He wants you to go:

Heal the sick, raise the dead, cleanse those who have
leprosy, drive out demons. Freely you have received; freely
give. Matthew 10:8 (NIV)

And this is what He says about what you need in your luggage:

Do not get any gold or silver or copper to take with you in your belts—no bag for the journey or extra shirt or sandals or a staff, for the worker is worth his keep. Matthew 10:9-10 (NIV)

Be the miracle that others need!

He's saying for us to be the miracle that others need. He's with us. We don't have to have any fancy Bible degree or beautiful words, we just need to speak life, encouragement and healing to those around us. We don't have to worry about the economy, for we are now in God's economy, and we can trust that God will supernaturally provide for our journey. You are worth your keep to the Lord so don't be afraid of the adventure ahead.

Pack Light

I love to travel. It's so fun to see different parts of the world and experience new customs and cultures. When I first started to travel, I was what I like to call a chronic over-packer! Can you relate? I would get anxious over what to bring and what to leave behind. I wanted to be prepared for every event and all kinds of weather and feel accepted in whatever culture I found myself in.

Here's the point: I'd pack out of fear thinking I wouldn't have everything that I needed when I got to my final destination. Do you ever feel like that spiritually? Sometimes I find myself fretting over where God's taking me, and I just don't think I have what it takes to make the journey. Sounds like Israel! They were packing their bags full of fear, anxiety, anger, disappointment, distrust, and those suitcases were too heavy to make the trip! Have you ever gotten up to the check-in counter at the airport and your bag was too heavy? It's humiliating.

True story: Once I was on a trip to Africa and our team had an overnight layover and stayed at a hotel at the airport. When we checked back into the South African airport, they had different weight requirements for their carry-on bags, and we had no idea until we reached the counter. We went to check in and all of our bags were overweight! We literally opened each of our suitcases and put on multiple layers of outfits to get the bags at the right weight. We looked ridiculous!

I think we look ridiculous to heaven at times with what we think is necessary for where God is taking us. One thing's for sure, if you have ever had to navigate airports, transportation and hotels, then you appreciate the ease of the journey when you pack light. No lost luggage, no waiting at baggage claim after a long flight, no throwing your back out trying to carry multiple suitcases at once! The list could go on and on.

Over the years, I have overcome my packing problems and perfected (for the most part) the way I travel. I have gone to Australia, Mozambique, Italy, and all over the US with just a carry-on! Don't worry, I will share all my secrets with you, but when I do, I want you to also hear them through a spiritual filter so you can know what is needed for your God-adventure!

Tip one: prepare. The first step to learning how to pack light is preparation. I will try on my outfits and take a picture of them so I don't have to be stressed about things that I can so easily take care of before I begin the trip. What can you do now that will take the pressure off later? You may not always have a Bible handy or available, so do you have the Word of God etched into your heart? When it's time, what will happen if you have unresolved disappointments lingering in your heart? Not only can disappointment be heavy, but it can also be hazardous. What about your finances? Are you setting some money aside, paying off debt and living frugally? When I feel directionless, I tend to overspend, but when I know I'm preparing for something, it's easy for me to say no to a new pair of shoes! As Benjamin Franklin once said, "Don't put off until tomorrow what you can accomplish today!" Prepare and know that you are going somewhere!

You might be reading this right now, and the problem is you don't know where God is taking you, and it's driving you crazy to be in this season of limbo, where you are waiting and you don't even know what you're waiting on! Seasons like this can challenge your purpose and identity. At times when busyness, titles, or community are taken away, we can question who we are and what God is doing, but don't reject what God has meant for us to enjoy. There's something special for you in this space, in the quiet. It's in the stillness we can visit the painful places that have been hidden in the hurry, so we can heal.

I want to encourage you in this time to prepare! God has not forgotten you. He is calling you to a preparation season. 2 Timothy 4:2 clearly says for us to "be prepared in season and out of season." Do not waste this space, my friend. This is an intentional appointment from the Lord, so treat it that way! Take time to create spiritual disciplines, invest in relationships, read, pray, write, and grow yourself for what's to come. This is not the time for you to Netflix, sulk, binge or be lazy! Be intentional.

I have a friend that keeps a carry-on packed by her door so when the Lord tells her to go somewhere, she's ready! Once God called her to go overseas and minister for six months, but she had a bag packed six months before she got the call! You'll never get this time back, and it's important for you to prepare so you can have what you need for the journey.

Tip two: think multipurpose and multifunctional. Layers are great. I look at my wardrobe and see how I can dress things up and down for whatever event I might walk into. As humans, we have layers of complexity that sometimes slow us down. Shedding layers to meet people where they are without fear of who you are can lead to beautiful, unexpected miraculous moments. That's one thing I so loved about my father-in-law. He had a testimony ready whether it was on an elevator ride, hospital stay, or platform. Without an ounce of shame or fear, he would smile the biggest smile you could ever see, shake your hand and say, "Hi, I'm Robert. I was a heroin addict and drug dealer, but God saved me." That's how I want to live. I want to be ready for the layers of God's goodness and grace to be shared with others.

God wants to use us when we think multifunctional. Meaning we're not bound to a title, plan or place, but instead, we can be used at any time and in any way. Over the years, I've made this mistake, thinking my identity was wrapped up in a position. As I've matured, I've realized that who I am is so much more important than seasonal salutations. I can wear them, but I'm also secure enough in who I am that when God calls me to leave them behind, I can. We are created by God, with the intention to be used for His expressed will, at any time, in any way. Every day is an adventure! Our roles, plans, and location may change, but our identity does not. It's secure in Christ no matter what He asks of us.

One day I was getting ready to drop my son off at his small group at the park. I had planned to go to the grocery store while he was there, but as I began to walk out the door, I heard the Holy Spirit whisper to me, "Take your anointing oil." I thought that was so odd and wondered how this grocery run may have me awkwardly anointing someone by the avocados!

Nevertheless, I put the oil in my purse and dropped my son off at the park. When I did, I received a text from a leader at my church, and she shared with me that she had just received a cancer diagnosis in her left knee. She asked for prayer because at that moment fear was trying to creep in. Again the Holy Spirit spoke, "Go to her house." I had never been to her apartment before and didn't even know if she would be there. Nevertheless, I looked her up in the church database and took a risk and just showed up unannounced. This is totally out of my character and comfort zone! When she answered the doorbell, she grabbed me and, through her tears, exclaimed, "You are here!"

Her house was filled with her small group, who had gathered to pray. A word of knowledge came, and I shared it with her, "There is no cancer in your body. God has already healed you. We are going to gather in agreement over this word, anoint you with oil and pray." It was a beautiful moment. The next day she went in to receive a treatment plan from her doctor, but after a scan, they told her that they didn't know what happened, but there was absolutely no cancer in her body! She knew exactly what happened, and so did we!

God is so good! He wants to use us in adventurous ways, but if we are so tied to our plan or our limited perspective of our roles, we will miss out on what He's doing! I could have had a fully stocked refrigerator as planned, but because I allowed God to interrupt my path and order my steps, I got to be a part of a miraculous moment! Stop restricting yourself from the adventurous life God has called you to because of small thinking! You are more than your stage of life. You are more than your season. You are more than a title. You are more than your mistakes. You are more! Step into your call by responding to the voice of God in your life.

During my season of homeschooling my kids, I shared with a mom about how God had called me at this particular time to step into their education. She told me that she couldn't hear God like that and concluded that she must not be on the same level with Christ as me. I looked at her and said, "I know you hear from God!" She was confused and asked me how. I asked her if she had ever been upset about something and prayed and felt peace. She said she had. I excitedly told her, "That's God speaking to you." God speaks to us in ways we can hear Him. I asked her if she had ever just felt that something was off with her boys and discovered from those promptings that something had happened. She said yes. "That's the Holy Spirit giving you insight," I exclaimed! The more we listen, the more we will hear. The more steps of obedience we take, the more God will entrust us with!

A scarce mentality will make us become Christians that hide and hoard instead of Christians that go and give.

Tip three: don't limit yourself and God. There will be times when you feel like you don't have what you need to go where you're going. When I'm packing, I always feel like I'm forgetting something, but now, I remind myself that I can buy whatever I need when I get there! Although my Amex may have a limit, my God does not! We're never going to be ready for what God wants us to do, but He's enough to fulfill His purpose through us! He is unlimited in His kindness, character, forgiveness, power, and resources. A scarce mentality will make us become Christians that hide and hoard instead of Christians that go

Stop over-preparing and instead walk in authority!

and give. The law of God is countercultural: the more we release, the more He releases to us. If we wait until we know it all, we will never do anything for Christ! Let's stop over-preparing and instead walk in authority!

Sometimes we reject God's plan because we disqualify His presence, as if He isn't enough for the miracle needed. Where the presence of God is, there is life, healing, freedom and provision! Go where He's going! God might not call you to show up unannounced at someone's house, but when we start listening to the Holy Spirit on the little things, He'll start to trust us with bigger things.

> *You, dear children, are from God and have*
> *overcome them, because the one who is in you*
> *is greater than the one who is in the world.*
> *1 John 4:4 (NIV)*

It's time for us to believe that the power of Christ lives in us! Where we go, God goes because He's with us and works through us! Do you realize that God watches over His Word to perform it (Jeremiah 1:12)? So we can trust that He will do what He says He will do. Know what you believe, and then let your actions follow it. If we believe that God is limited, then we will be cautious of our time, prayers, and requests, but if we understand that He is limitless, we will operate as if we're never a bother to Him. We'll believe that He cares about the details of our lives, and we'll get radical with our prayers and actions.

Tip four: make room for new! When I'm struggling with whether or not to leave something behind or take it with me, I remind myself that if I'm too bogged down and overpacked, I won't have any room for something new to bring home from my journey. I love to bring home my best finds, especially when I travel to Italy! Let's not hold on to things that limit our capacity for what's next. If I pack offense, unforgiveness, fear or regret, I'm not going to get very far with that heavy load! God wants to redeem what's behind us and prosper what's ahead of us, but if we are too tied down and can't let it go, we will miss our flight. Leave it behind! I promise what's ahead is so much more worthy of your space, time and attention.

Leave It Behind

Here's a look at some of the things I've left behind and am careful to not pick back up in my latest travels: hurts, disappointments, chaos, toxic relationships, titles, bad habits, negative self-talk, fear, people's expectations, insecurity, bad attitudes, mistakes and distrust. I've tried them all on, and frankly, they looked awful on me! I know what's deserving of the trip God has me on, and I frankly don't have use for these worn-out items any longer.

My bags are light because what God desires for me to bring doesn't take a lot of space. Faith is one of those things I can't possibly leave behind, and as we learned in the last chapter, it's as small as a mustard seed! Once planted, seeds grow. In the same way, my faith has grown through the community I've chosen to plant in. I have women in my circle of friends whose faith ignites me to speak the impossible into existence. If your friend group only sits around with negative talk and useless offenses, it's time to get a new circle! My friend often says if you don't like your harvest then change your seed.

I'm taking with me sharpening friendships that challenge me to expand my heart for all God is up to. If you are the smartest, brightest, most faith-filled person in your sphere of influence, you aren't going to build anything. I bring life to my friends, but they also bring life to me through encouragement and accountability. They walk beside me and are not a burden to my destiny or a stumbling block to my faith, they enlarge my vision. Grow your circle and they will grow you!

Grow your circle and they will grow you!

God cares about bringing you friends to help you get where you are going. They won't be cheap commodities to be used and exchanged upon convenience, they will be true investors to your future and companions to your soul. They will care about you, not your title. They will see you and support you, just as you will serve them. Joshua had Moses and Caleb alongside him to face every battle and walk through every personal challenge. They made each other better.

It reminds me of birds and how they travel in packs to provide safety and provision. Do you know that birds can be found on the land, sea and fresh water, and in virtually every habitat, from the lowest deserts to the highest mountains? This shows us that God cares for us even in the harshest environments! God gives forethought to our needs, so we can take with us His promises, knowing that we are more valuable to Him than birds.

God gives forethought to our needs.

Look at the birds of the air, for they neither sow nor
reap nor gather into barns; yet your heavenly Father
feeds them. Are you not of more value than they?
Matthew 6:26 (NKJV)

God's provision not only follows us, but it's also waiting on us! David pens it like this in Psalm 139:7-12 (NIV):

God's provision not only follows us, but it's also waiting on us!

Where can I go from your Spirit?
Where can I flee from your presence?
If I go up to the heavens, you are there;
if I make my bed in the depths, you are there.
If I rise on the wings of the dawn,
if I settle on the far side of the sea,
even there your hand will guide me,
your right hand will hold me fast.
If I say, "Surely the darkness will hide me
and the light become night around me,"
even the darkness will not be dark to you;
the night will shine like the day,
for darkness is as light to you.

We can be courageous in our adventures, no matter what dark things we may encounter, because the light of Christ is guiding our way. My list of things I'm taking is quite long, but at the same time so light. How about you? What will you leave behind? What will you take with you? Plan now to pack your bags by cleaning out the closet of your life. You don't need so much of what's there, cluttering up and even hiding some of your best pieces.

Adventure

As we come to a close of this book, I hope to impart into you an adventurous spirit. For some, it can be a hard thing to step into because we are so used to sticking to a tight plan and not giving margin for the unexpected, but for others, it's reigniting a flame of that adventurous girl we once were in our youth. Being a Christian, if you do it right, is anything but dull and boring. Joshua died and was buried in the land of his dreams. He left nothing undone. He finished what was started!

You have a choice of who you become, but the choice isn't always clear. You may be reading this right now thinking, "How did I get here?" At one juncture of your life, you may have been the most adventurous faith-filled person around, but now, you are doing good if you pray for your lunch before eating it! Maybe you are playing life too safe. If you go to church, you go late and leave early. If you pray, it's not with conviction or belief. You can't remember the last time you shared Jesus with someone. It's time to wake up! We are on the shortest side of eternity: heaven is forever, but our lives here on earth are just a vapor, so let's make life count!

There's nothing adventurous about staying stuck in insecurity, fear or the past. There is no excitement or adrenaline found in sulking over what you lost or what you would do differently either. Joshua didn't take one big step, he took a bunch of small steps of faith along the way. Some steps he missed, but he didn't stop stepping. It's time to take a step again. Even if you misstep, at least you tried, and you can have a valuable lesson learned to help you with your next step!

God put this book in my heart about ten years before I wrote it. After about five years, I had a twenty-four-hour period where I felt so condemned by these thoughts around it:

- ♥ I've done nothing with what God asked me to do.
- ♥ I didn't hear from God. This must have been my dream, not His.
- ♥ I did something wrong, and that's why God can't use me in this way.

The next day as I was leaving work, I rolled down my passenger window to a man who looked lost. I gave him some directions, and he proceeded to cross his arms and rest them on the window seal looking at me intently. With confidence and clarity, he said to me, "I see that you are going to write a book. The Holy Spirit is going to wake you up, and as you put your hands on your computer, He will anoint you and the words will flow through your fingers as you type." He continued to tell me specific details about this book and more. He shared with me more than the Lord had ever revealed to me around this adventurous dream, then just walked away as if it were nothing. I had never seen him before, and I haven't seen him since. I went home and laid prostrate on the floor, crying out to God thanking Him for confirming His Word to me. None of those accusations against me were true. It just wasn't God's timing for the dream He had placed in me. He was still writing the words in this book through the development of my heart.

Just because something doesn't immediately work out or you make a mistake along the way doesn't mean you aren't meant to do it. I haven't stopped getting on planes just because I made several wrong choices about my travel! My mistakes are not my identity. I know who I am. I know that even when I experience failure,

My mistakes are not my identity.

God's got an even bigger success in store with my next steps with Him. It's time for your thoughts about yourself to come up a notch. It's time to be who God has called you to be. You can be more and do more than you think. Every adventure starts with a first step. You don't know how it will start, and you don't know how it will end, but you can be sure that if you go on the adventure, God will go with you and bring light to the path to guide you the right way.

It's time for your thoughts about yourself to come up a notch.

Joshua lived an adventurous life, chasing his dream by following the plan and will of God. This *victorious* adventure came with:

- ♥ Rejection
- ♥ Betrayal
- ♥ Lies
- ♥ Deceit
- ♥ Delays
- ♥ Deaths
- ♥ Battles
- ♥ Wounds

Joshua was around forty when he left his life of slavery in Egypt, he was around eighty when he began his conquest to inhabit the Promise Land, and he was one hundred and ten when he went to heaven. There was no get rich quick scheme, just hard work, ups and downs, disappointments and victories and the presence of God leading the way through it all. He left nothing undone despite the challenges faced. He lived a full life inhabiting his promise. He received his reward.

I'll leave you with these last words from Joshua as you step into a posture of an adventurous life, fully surrendered to the Lord:

It was the Lord our God himself who brought us and our parents up out of Egypt, from that land of slavery, and performed those great signs before our eyes.

He protected us on our entire journey and among all the nations through which we traveled. Joshua 24:17 (NIV)

*Now I am about to go the way of all the earth. You know with all your heart and soul that **not one of all the good promises the Lord your God gave you has failed.** Joshua 23:14 (NIV)*

Every promise will be fulfilled; not one will fail. **You are not who you think you are,** *you are who God says you are.* So *think different,* my friend. *Break cycles* and *be confident.*

Conclusion
Dare to Believe

My last encouragement to you, as you learn who you are in Christ, is to dare to believe that you are more than what you see! That reflection that has been intimidating you can now do what a mirror is supposed to do: aid you. It will show you places where you are healed and places that have the opportunity to become whole. It will be a place where you can give up the dim view of yourself that has clouded your thoughts for far too long, and maybe, just maybe, for the first time you see what God sees.

I opened this book talking about my thirtieth birthday and its dread. Now as we close, I want to share my fortieth birthday experience in hopes that you can see that it's possible to reclaim your identity and embrace all that God has created you to be.

I have some really great memories from my childhood, but as you know, looking back I often had feelings of rejection and humiliation. I have a wonderful family whom I adore, and I considered us to be very close in this season of our lives. Still, at family gatherings, I often found myself feeling like an outsider, insignificant and withdrawn.

For whatever reason, I had never prayed about this before, so I began to ask God to redeem my perspective, even to show me good memories I had forgotten, in hopes of shifting my thinking so I would no longer go back to places of pain, but instead, enjoy the gift of family the Lord has given me. One of the cool things about God is that He not only hears us, but He wants to do exceedingly above what we ask for. I never could have guessed how this would all play out, but let's just say my fortieth birthday was one for the books!

My amazing husband, amid COVID, gave me a surprise progressive birthday that lasted twenty-four hours! That's right, twenty-four hours. I was taken to a location where a few of my favorite people would be to spend some quality time together, and then I would be given a clue to take me to my next destination. It started with dinner with my sisters and some of my closest friends.

To be honest, I was expecting my sisters to tell embarrassing stories of my youth. I had a little dread as I anxiously thought about what they might share and my perception of how my sisters viewed me. Then, my sister began to share how I had touched her life on many different occasions, forgiven things we had never discussed and strengthened her faith through my walk with the Lord. At that moment the Lord declared to me,

"You will not be humiliated or remember the shame of your youth" (Isaiah 54:4.) Then, they presented me with a pair of diamond earrings! What?! Who does that? As they gave them to me, the Lord impressed on me, "You are valuable" (Matthew 10:31).

I could have just been done with my birthday after that, but it wasn't over, it had just begun. The next day, my little sister and mom showed up to take me for a pedicure. As we talked, laughed and were pampered, the tears I once cried were poured out and used to make the rocky journey I had walked smooth with beautiful feet and good tidings (Romans 10:15).

Another clue read, "You will spend an hour with someone very special to you." As I drove up to the house, my dad was standing there with his tennis shoes on ready for a brisk walk. Growing up my dad would spend countless hours going on walks with my sister as they would talk about everything under the sun, but I was always left at home, left with thoughts that I wasn't worthy of my father's time, affection or attention. No matter what I felt growing up, those sentiments are not a true reflection of the relationship we had built in my adult years. During that walk, the Lord declared to me, "You are your father's delight" (Psalm 147:11).

I was driven to lunch, and my pastors were there to share a favorite meal with my husband and me. For eighteen years they saw purpose and potential in me, things I could never envision for myself. They were patient with me through every awkward moment of growth and stretching. Their love never wavered no matter the difficulty of the seasons we had stewarded together. They handed me a box, and in it was a gold necklace stamped "I am loved." God marked me as loved through their care for me (1 John 4:7).

On and on the clues came and went with so many things I hold dear to my heart, and as we drove up for the finale, I began to cry. At the gate of my best friend's house, the Lord reminded me of the refuge He had built for me there. I had once felt as though I wasn't deserving of friends and that once I was truly known, I would be trashed. "Who could love me?" I would think. But there, on that very property, I was fully known and fully loved. Not only is God a friend to the friendless, but He also gives you friends that build a safe place to let down all guards and in complete transparency experience true love, devotion and closeness. My parents, sisters, brothers-in-law, nieces, nephew and adopted family lined the driveway with sparklers as we drove in. The Lord declared over me, "You are celebrated" (Zephaniah 3:17).

As if the day hadn't been enough, I began to open the most thoughtful gift I've ever received. Framed in silver trim and written in the shape of a heart, it said, "40 Things We Love About You." Each member of my tribe had written the way they see me: kind, loyal, graceful, solution-giver, generous, encourager, playful, passionate, truth-giver and cheerleader to others, just to name a few. As I read these words, I realized

Who you were, is not who you are!

that, like Joshua, God wasn't interested in erasing my past, He had redeemed it. Who I was, is not who I am. What I experienced happened to me, but it's not happening now. My view of myself was not the view others held. My mistakes had not overshadowed the goodness of God in my life. I no longer have to relive what is behind me.

The Lord, in His kindness, wanted to show me how silly that little view I had of myself was and how it reflected a false narrative of the true experience and impact my life has had on those around me. God has redeemed me, my relationships and my story for His glory. I'm not some small person sitting in the background, insignificant and defeated. No, my life is a living testimony of rags to riches! I was born a slave, but now I ride first class into every God-adventure knowing I'm a kingdom heir.

With a redeemed perspective, my eyes can spend less attention on the mirror of my own life and more attention on being a mirror for others, helping them to see what God sees. Confident and secure, we can reverse the direction of the image reflected by shining light on the viewer and removing obstacles that were behind them for clarity of what's ahead. Then, with the observer's own eyes, they can correctly perceive and truly embrace that they are not who they were. What happened to them doesn't have to be a continuing saga of emotional drama pulling them away from the beautiful reflection the Lord wants to shine a light on.

My prayer is that you, too, can now look into the mirror of your life and see what God sees. Give that girl you see the chance she's been dying for. Remind her to: be whole, be smart, be trustworthy, be consistent, be confident, be redeemed, be strong and courageous, be bold, be obedient, be coachable, be you, be alert, and be adventurous.

This earthly life is too short to spend it second-guessing God's purpose in your life. He is challenging you to trust Him. He's calling you out into the waters where miracles happen. He's confirming to you that you will see your God-dreams come to pass because God, the Dream Giver, will be walking with you. Pack your bag, girl, for you are never going back to the mundane. God has so much more in store!

You are not who you think you are!

Think different. Break cycles. Be confident.

Acknowledgements

To Katie Chambers of Beacon Point LLC: Thank you for your thought-provoking questions that helped me put words to my experiences. Your coaching and input strengthened the form and substance of this book. I'm grateful that God put you in my path to assist me in birthing this dream through your editing expertise and dedication to excellence.

To Daniel Gonzales: Not only are you a supportive husband, but you are also my secret ingredient to success. Thank you for making a book cover that pulled together the essence of this book. There is truly nothing you cannot do. Thank you for choosing to do this with me.

About the Author

Celeste Gonzales holds many titles—wife, mother, daughter, preacher's kid, sister, friend, author and pastor to name a few—but she is way more than a title. At heart, she is a lover of Jesus and His people. She's devoted to her family, passionate about the Word of God, the first call to her friends in a time of need, a shopping buddy when her schedule allows, a cook to unexpected dinner guests, a great hugger when you just need a warm embrace and wise counsel to point you in the right direction.

Following her life's mission, to honor God by being obedient in both the small and big things, she passionately ministers to thousands of women across the globe, seeing them come to know Jesus and unashamedly walk in freedom. Celeste comes alive when sharing the gospel to God's girls, whether in the states, on the mission field, in prisons or one on one over tea or dinner. With over a decade of full-time ministry experience, Celeste is an accomplished communicator, conference director and Women's Pastor. She combines her life experience and gut-wrenching vulnerability with epic Bible tales and humorous wit to spur you on to your God-call. She currently serves on the pastoral team at Celebration Church, in Austin, Texas, where she resides. Celeste is happiest when she's with her husband, Daniel of nineteen years, and their three kiddos: Syrena, Luke and Kya.

Celeste is just an ordinary girl living an extraordinary life.

Connect with Celeste:

Website: www.celestegonzales.com
Instagram: @celesteadores
Facebook: https://www.facebook.com/shoutatceleste

Endnotes

1. "Shame," Wikipedia, last modified May 18, 2022, https://en.wikipedia.org/wiki/Shame.

2. Merriam-Webster, s.v. "guilt," accessed June 2022, https://www.merriam-webster.com/dictionary/guilt.

3. Kenneth Barker, ed., The NIV Study Bible Fully Revised (Michigan: Zondervan, 1985), 209.

4. Merriam-Webster, s.v. "entrust," accessed June 2022, https://www.merriam-webster.com/dictionary/entrust.

5. Merriam-Webster, s.v. "prune," accessed June 2022, https://www.merriam-webster.com/dictionary/prune.

6. W.L. Walker, "Confidence," Bible History, Maps, Images and Archeology, accessed June 2022, https://bible-history.com/isbe/c/confidence/.

7. Merriam-Webster, s.v. "confidant," accessed June 2022, https://www.merriam-webster.com/dictionary/confidant.

8. Merriam-Webster, s.v. "vulnerable," accessed June 2022, https://www.merriam-webster.com/dictionary/vulnerable.

9. Merriam-Webster, s.v. "authenticity," accessed June 2022, https://www.merriam-webster.com/dictionary/authenticity.

10. "The Gut-Brain Connection: The relationship to emotions and managing stress," Mind and Body Words, accessed June 2022, https://mindandbodyworks.com/the-gut-brain-connection-the-relationship-to-emotions-and-managing-stress/.

11. Merriam-Webster, s.v. "redeem," accessed June 2022, https://www.merriam-webster.com/dictionary/redeem.

12. Doron Kornbluth and Seth Aronstam, "Jericho," Chabad.org, accessed June 2022, https://www.chabad.org/library/article_cdo/aid/4417327/jewish/Jericho.htm.

13. "Marion Jones," Wikipedia, last updated May 21, 2022, https://en.wikipedia.org/wiki/Marion_Jones.

14. Tom Henschel, "Creating New Behaviors," The Look and Sound of Leadership, podcast audio, May 2013, https://essentialcomm.com/podcast/creating-new-behaviors/.

15. Wendy Wisner, "Joshua Name Meaning," VeryWell Family, updated August 5, 2021, https://www.verywellfamily.com/joshua-name-meaning-origin-popularity-5180223.

16. Doug Hershey, "Yeshua: The Meaning of the Hebrew Name of Jesus," Fellowship of Israel Related Ministries, December 22, 2015, https://firmisrael.org/learn/who-is-yeshua-meaning-of-hebrew-name-jesus/.

17. Merriam-Webster, s.v. "enjoy," accessed June 2022, https://www.merriam-webster.com/dictionary/enjoy.

18. Merriam-Webster, s.v. "reject," accessed June 2022, https://www.merriam-webster.com/dictionary/reject.

Made in the USA
Columbia, SC
11 September 2022